The Pivotal Year

How Freshmen Can Become Sophomores

Robert L. Marshall

A SCARECROWEDUCATION BOOK

The Scarecrow Press, Inc.
Lanham, Maryland, and Oxford
2003

i 0810847167

Published in the United States of America
by ScarecrowEducation
An imprint of The Rowman & Littlefield Publishing Group, Inc.
4501 Forbes Boulevard, Suite 200, Lanham, Maryland 20706
www.scarecroweducation.com

PO Box 317
Oxford
OX2 9RU, UK

British Library Cataloguing in Publication Information Available

Library of Congress Cataloging-in-Publication Data

Marshall, Robert L. (Robert Lester), 1953–
  The pivotal year : how freshman can become sophomores / Robert L.
Marshall.
     p. cm.
"A ScarecrowEducation book."
Includes bibliographical references and index.
  ISBN 0-8108-4716-7 (pbk. : alk. paper)
  1. Ninth grade (Education)—United States. 2. Academic achievement—
United States. 3. Promotion (School)—United States. 4. Grade repetition—
United States. I. Title.
  LB1629.79th .M37 2003
  373.238—dc21
                                                              2002154950

∞™ The paper used in this publication meets the minimum requirements of
American National Standard for Information Sciences—Permanence of
Paper for Printed Library Materials, ANSI/NISO Z39.48-1992.
Manufactured in the United States of America.

Contents

CHAPTER 1

The Case of Ninth-Grade Failure

President George W. Bush and his national education advisors have coined the phrase "No Child Left Behind." Though this is a noble vision at the national level, the reality is that children are being left behind: not at the first or third grade but largely at the ninth-grade level. Thousands of children are left behind every year due to the current structure and problems associated with the transition from middle school/junior high to high school. In many states, the number one grade for retention is grade nine. Ninth graders in America's schools are at particular risk of failure. More students repeat ninth grade than any other grade, and more decide to drop out of school during or at the end of their ninth-grade year than at any other time (Texas Center for Educational Research, 2002).

Over the past decade, very little progress has been made to alleviate the high failures and graduation rate deficits that leave many children behind without a future of hope or chance for prosperity. A few select schools address the problem of high failures at the ninth grade and have made progressive strides toward success; however, numbers tell us that not enough is being done to make a much-needed nationwide impact.

We know why students are failing, we know what they are failing, and we know, through research, that retention in the same grade helps very little. So why are so many students still being retained in the ninth grade?

The ninth grade for many students marks the beginning of success or failure in their school careers; it is the first time that each course they take counts for something more than just "seat time" in a classroom.

The successful student must pass courses to accumulate the credits necessary to graduate from high school or to take the course over again if he or she fails to pass. Herein lies the problem: the unsuccessful ninth-grade student remains in the ninth grade for another year, taking the same courses again while becoming a year older and looking more seriously at the alternative of dropping out of school. The most significant problem facing our society is the number of students who fail to graduate from high school. Indeed, it is estimated that between 33 and 35 percent of the students who enter the ninth grade will fail to graduate four years later.

The ninth grade is the place where "the rubber meets the road," so to speak, and many students lack sufficient social and academic skills to succeed in the instructional environment of public high schools. These young people are at an awkward stage of adolescence, yet they face the most demanding and drastic changes in their careers as students. Ninth-grade students face less curriculum flexibility and limited scheduling flexibility. The individuals most likely to drop out before completing the ninth grade are those who have had attendance, discipline, and/or academic problems in the past, possibly from the beginning of their school careers (Ascher, 1987). Failure at the ninth-grade level has significantly greater implications than in earlier school years because students must accumulate a set number of credits to avoid retention.

Having worked as an administrator in five school districts and conducted research in several others, there seems to be a common problem among many school districts: 10 to 50 percent of the students in the ninth grade are retained each year. In the state of Texas, there were 350,864 students (8.9 percent of the total student population) enrolled in the ninth grade and 212,773 students (5.4 percent of the total student population) enrolled in the twelfth grade in the 1998–1999 school year. This calculates to a difference of 138,091 students between these grade levels. In fact, each group between these grade levels suffers a considerable loss as well, with 273,262 students enrolled in the tenth grade, a difference of 77,602 students between ninth and tenth grade. The differential continues the trend when comparing ninth grade to eleventh grade, with 240,860 students and a difference of 110,004 students. In one large urban district, there were 18,236 freshmen and 9,851 seniors, or a 54 percent graduation rate, and in another area of the state the same

Table 1.1.   State of Texas Enrollment Figures Grades 9–12, Taken from Texas
Education Agency Public Education Information Management System (PEIMS) Data

Year	9th	10th	11th	12th	*Difference/%
1995–1996	335,819	255,132	213,714	186,229	149,590/44.5%
1996–1997	343,923	264,289	225,833	195,291	148,623/43.2%
1997–1998	348,093	270,634	234,187	207,226	140,867/40.5%
1998–1999	350,864	273,262	240,860	212,773	138,091/39.4%

*Difference is calculated by subtracting the twelfth-grade figure from the ninth-grade figure and the per-
   cent is acquired by dividing the difference by the ninth-grade number (example: 149,590/335,819 =
   44.5%).

scenario applies in another large district, with 14,838 in the ninth
grade and 6,138 in the twelfth grade, or a 41.34 percent graduation rate.
Nationwide figures for the United States do not get any better, with
3,934,899 students in the ninth grade and 2,781,701 enrolled in the
twelfth grade, a difference of 1,153,198, in 1998–1999. With these astronomical attrition rates of students between ninth and twelfth grade,
there is something wrong with the system. Yet very little effort or attention is being expended to alleviate this problem. Tables 1.1 and 1.2
paint a vivid picture of the devastating numbers and percentages of students who are left behind with little hope for future success in life.

A profile of the data for a Texas public school dropout shows a dropout
as most likely to be Hispanic, male, overage for the grade by at least one
year, and in the ninth or tenth grade when leaving school. More than 80
percent of students who left school in the 1996–1997 school year were
overage for the grade. Males were more likely to drop out than females.
The largest number of dropouts was found in ninth grade. The highest
dropout rate, however, was found among twelfth graders. Also, less than
40 percent of 1996–1997 dropouts were identified as at risk of dropping
out of school the year they dropped out (Texas Education Agency, 1998).

Table 1.2.   United States Enrollment Figures Grades 9–12

Year	9th	10th	11th	12th	*Difference/%
1996–1997	3,792,818	3,316,015	2,925,139	2,581,941	1,210,877/32%
1997–1998	3,818,929	3,376,595	2,972,004	2,673,067	1,145,862/30%
1998–1999	3,856,100	3,381,772	3,018,065	2,723,707	1,132,393/29%
1999–2000	3,934,899	3,415,425	3,033,980	2,781,701	1,153,198/29%

*Difference is calculated by subtracting the twelfth-grade figure from the ninth-grade figure and the per-
   cent is acquired by dividing the difference by the ninth-grade number (example: 1,210,877/3,792,818
   = 32%).

Texas is not in sole possession of the problem of ninth-grade failure or high dropout rates. In a recent study by Chute, in Pittsburgh, Pennsylvania, the number of ninth graders retained is dramatically near those in Texas. Nearly one-fourth of ninth graders—23.4 percent—did not pass enough courses to be promoted to the tenth grade at the end of the 1997–1998 school year. The statistics for ninth grade at the end of the 1997–1998 school year in Pittsburgh show some of the risks students face:

- The lowest attendance in any grade level was in ninth grade. The average attendance was 78 percent compared with 92.5 percent in first grade and 80.9 percent in twelfth grade. And this is a drop from the 86.3 percent attendance recorded for eighth grade.
- The largest percentage of failing grades (25.5 percent) was in ninth grade, but only 5.7 percent of the grades in eighth grade were failing grades.
- The highest percentage of overage students was in the ninth grade. Nearly 14 percent of ninth graders were at least 16.5 years old at the end of the school year.
- About one in three (33.8 percent) of all ninth graders was suspended out of school, less than the district high of 37 percent in eighth grade. (Chute, 1999)

A common contributing factor to student difficulty in the first year of high school is the lack of success a student experiences before grade nine. Students who have been retained in the same grade one or more times are likely candidates for continuation of the same. If the system turns its head and allows the students to slip through the cracks, the trend of apathy and failure will not change to any significant degree. Grade-level retention is one of the most common interventions of our educational system. The relationship of grade retention to high-school dropouts has been noted by a plethora of research studies in the past. In addition, a considerable amount of research supports the generalization that grade repeaters are 20 to 30 percent more likely to drop out of school prior to graduation than are on-grade-level classmates with similar achievement levels. It is further noted that students who are retained experience greater personal and scholastic adjustments (Hagborg and Masella, 1991).

According to the Texas Commissioner of Education, Jim Nelson, students in danger of dropping out of school believe they cannot successfully complete school because they have too many problems. Furthermore, they may have other family members who have dropped out of school. These students are only continuing a family tradition that is not looked on as anything other than an ordinary, acceptable turn of events. However, it should be looked on by teachers, administrators, and parents as a crisis in the making, and the world of education should stop in its tracks until these young people are back in school working toward completion of a high-school education.

Institutional and individual factors associated with the decision to leave school are the focus of much research. Many of these characteristics are beyond anyone's control and are measured late in a student's school career. Some of the factors associated with a student's decision to exit the educational process are out of the educators' reach, and any interventions that might alleviate such a decision come much too late in the progression of life's events to make significant progress. Research by Finn in 1989 describes two models for understanding dropping out as a developmental process that may begin in the earliest grades. The frustration–self-esteem model identifies school failure as the starting point in a cycle that ends in a student's dropping out. A participation–identification model focuses on involvement and participation and has behavioral as well as emotional components. Moreover, the correlates of dropping out of school—problem behaviors, skipping class and truancy, disruptive behavior in the classroom, and juvenile delinquency—are only a small part of a problem that usually starts early in a child's school career. Every dialogue about dropping out, attendance problems, disruptive behavior, or delinquency usually equates to a strong relationship between the associated factors. These problem behaviors are all associated with poor academic performance, as is dropping out. Finn contends that "identification" and "participation" are basic components for an alternative model of dropping out. The extent to which a youngster identifies with and participates in school is related to such behaviors as absenteeism, dropout, and delinquency. Unfortunately, alienation and withdrawal are characteristics that define dropouts and are the basis of other behaviors that result in the student's rejecting or being rejected by the school (Finn, 1989).

A recent research report by the Texas Education Agency identified a set of characteristics related to grade retention among Texas students. Students who are male, are members of minority groups, are economically disadvantaged, have limited English proficiency, receive special education services, or are overage for their grade are retained more often than other students. Thus, even students who repeat ninth grade and remain in school continue to be at increased risk of failure (Texas Center for Educational Research, 2002).

Longitudinal research has shown that the predominant contributing factor to students leaving school is the grade-level education of their mother. This fact is further supported by a recent study of South Texas dropouts in 1999 in which twenty students who made the decision to leave school were surveyed and interviewed. Of the twenty students in the study, the data showed that only three fathers and four mothers were high-school graduates (Mireles, 1999).

In current field practice, many educators move students through the educational system with little regard to individual needs; this approach contributes to the failure of far too many students. Furthermore, the student–teacher relationship at the ninth grade is weakened by the fragmented organizational structure of the school as teachers specialize in subject-content areas (Wells, 1989). We must change our paradigm to something other than what we currently do to make students successful in school. Through field-based observation, practical experience, and literary research, some practices have been discovered that can be implemented to increase the success of students who are experiencing difficulty in school.

Just who is responsible for the success of the student when the classroom door closes tight? Is it the parent? Is it the principal, or better yet, the superintendent? When the classroom door closes, the only help one receives comes from the confines of that classroom. The teacher holds the key to success and controls the conditions for success inside the classroom. In addition, when the door is closed, only the teacher and the students are left to create the motivation to succeed and breed the success that facilitates further successes that move students beyond the transition year in high school or any other grade in school, for that matter.

This is not to say that the teacher is the only one who can have an effect on student success. It truly takes an entire support team to be persistent enough to take students to a higher level of academic performance than even they think is possible. Grade-level teams, counselors, administrators, students, and parents must all become a team to ensure student success at this level. When one of those members is not working, the others have to pull together to assist the student in transition. Even with all this in mind, it is clear that not every student will be saved and not every student can be successful in our current system; however, more students can be saved than the figures are showing. It was once said by a staff development consultant, "I know that Jesus Christ did not save everyone." He then went on to say to the faculty and staff, "Even though he didn't save everyone, he saved more than you people are saving from the numbers I see."

The astronomical figures, outlined earlier in this chapter, are a result of accepting that a certain number of students will fail and that the diversity of the student backgrounds and the problems associated with life outside of school is just too much to overcome. A group of caring, supportive, and driven teachers can make a difference with the support and flexibility of the administration. What it will take is those individuals standing together to say they want training related to these problems, want and need telephones in their classrooms, want the support of administration, and want to somehow change the number of students who are being retained in the ninth grade by doing whatever it takes.

CONCLUSION

Retention of ninth-grade students is a crisis in American public schools. We have a predetermined prophecy that perpetuates failure at this grade level, which fosters high dropout rates of thousands of students every year. In times past, society absorbed the undereducated and students that lacked a high-school diploma. Today the undereducated dropout becomes a social threat in most cases. Moreover, as we move through the highly technical information age into the biotechnical age, the need for highly qualified people with lifelong learning abilities will become even more profound. We can no longer continue

Determine your own trend of ninth-grade student success with the following table:					
Year	9th	10th	11th	12th	*Difference/%
1994–1995	_____	_____	_____	_____	_____/_____
1995–1996	_____	_____	_____	_____	_____/_____
1996–1997	_____	_____	_____	_____	_____/_____
1997–1998	_____	_____	_____	_____	_____/_____
1998–1999	_____	_____	_____	_____	_____/_____
1999–2000	_____	_____	_____	_____	_____/_____
2000–2001	_____	_____	_____	_____	_____/_____
2001–2002	_____	_____	_____	_____	_____/_____

Enter actual enrollment numbers for each grade level for each year to determine the differences in percent between ninth- and twelfth-grade students for each year.

*Difference is calculated by subtracting the twelfth-grade figure from the ninth-grade figure and the percent is acquired by dividing the difference by the ninth-grade number (example: 149,590/335,819 = 44.5%).

Figure 1.1.   *Hypothetical High-School Longitudinal Graduation Rate*

the support of a school system that fails children at the current rates seen in the majority of our large urban and suburban high schools across this great nation.

Taking the initiative to change the pattern of failure by thinking outside the traditional educational box is essential to change the pattern. A good first step is to look at the data, develop a plan, and implement that plan with passion (figure 1.1). We should leave no stone unturned in an effort to find what works to dramatically improve ninth-grade transition and success for our schools, communities, and children.

REFERENCES

Ascher, C. (1987). The ninth grade—a precarious time for the potential dropout. *ERIC Digest* 34, ED284 922. New York: ERIC Clearinghouse on Urban Education.

Chute, E. (1999). Back to school: Ninth grade proves to be a pivotal year for youths. *Pittsburgh Post-Gazette.* Available online at www.postgazette.com/regionstate/19990824ninth3.asp [accessed October 3, 2002].

Finn, J. D. (1989). Withdrawing from school. *Review of Educational Research* 59: 117–142.

Hagborg, W. J., and G. Masella. (1991). A follow-up study of high school students with a history of grade retention. *Psychology in the Schools* 28: 310.

Mireles, A. (1999). *Factors associated with student dropouts as perceived by counselors, teachers, and students, in selected South Texas school districts.* Unpublished dissertation at Texas A&M University–Kingsville, Texas.

Texas Center for Educational Research. (2002). At-risk students and the transition to high school: Texas' efforts to support ninth grade success. Austin, Tex.

Texas Education Agency. (1998). 1996–97 Texas public school dropout report (GE8-601-05). Austin, Tex.

Wells, A. S. (1989). Middle school education—The critical link in dropout prevention. ERIC Document Reproduction Service, no. ED311148.

ADDITIONAL WEB RESOURCES

National Center for Educational Statistics. "Dropout Report. Public High School Dropouts and Completers from the Common Core of Data: School Years 1991–92 through 1997–98." nces.ed.gov/pubsearch/pubsinfo. asp?pubid=2002317. "This report presents dropout and four-year high-school completion rates by state. Data is from the Common Core of Data collection. Dropout and completion-rate data are broken out by state, race/ethnicity, grade, and locale."

U.S. Department of Education. "High School Dropout Rates." www.ed.gov/pubs/OR/ConsumerGuides/dropout.html. "National Institute on the Education of At-Risk Students presents a series of questions and answers related to dropout rates and reporting practices across the nation."

National Center for Educational Statistics. "A Comparison of High School Dropout Rates in 1982–1992." nces.ed.gov/pubsearch/pubsinfo.asp?pubid= 96893. "Access an Acrobat Reader format of a report that examines the changing demographics of high-school students over the last decade and investigates the impact these changes may have had on high-school dropout rates."

Woods, E. Gregory. "Reducing the Dropout Rate." School Improvement Research Series. www.nwrel.org/scpd/c017.html. "A quality report on the progress toward higher graduation rates in America. This website provides a literature review on dropouts, solutions, and strategies to increase graduation rates in the nation's schools."

Pantleo, Sam J. "Program to Reduce Failure Rates of Ninth Grade Students." ericeece.org/pubs/digests/ed-cite/ed358391.html. "This report outlines the step necessary for developing and implementing a plan for curtailing ninth-grade failure rates in high schools with populations from 1,000 to 1,800 students."

Texas Education Agency. "Ninth Grade Success Initiative." www.tea.state.tx. us/curriculum/9gsi.html. "The Texas Education Agency provides a series of reports, applications, and evaluation forms on this site for the convenience of school administrators in Texas who are managing a ninth-grade initiative grant."

Texas Education Agency. "Student Success Initiatives: A Parent Guide to Testing Requirements." www.tea.state.tx.us/curriculum/ssi.html. "The Texas Education Agency provides clarification for the Student Success Initiative and information in the form of questions and answers for parents about the new process and standards for testing students."

Policy Studies Associates. "Implementing Schoolwide Programs: An Idea Book on Planning." www.ed.gov/pubs/Idea_Planning/title.html. "This report describes the process and provides resources for planning and evaluating programs in schools."

CHAPTER 2

Determining the Cause

Across the state of Texas and many others, grade nine is the number one grade failed, while across the nation, grade one leads the list. Teachers and other educators have grounded feelings about how to teach and how to motivate students to achieve; however, a common vision, mission, and attitude toward reducing failure must be reached before progress can be made.

Southern Regional Education Board (SREB) research provides extensive proof of the need for measures to be taken to help ease the transition of students to and through ninth grade. Among the compelling statistics they have released are the following:

- More students fail ninth grade than any other grade of school.
- Poor and minority students are twice as likely as others to be retained.
- Students who repeat at least one year are three times more likely to drop out of school than students who have not failed a grade.
- Sixty percent of students with multiple risk factors in eighth grade graduate from high school on time compared to 90 percent of other students.
- Career-bound students who take college preparatory (CP) courses in high school average 16 points higher on the *High Schools That Work* assessment than their counterparts in practical-level classes.
- The performance of students in Algebra I is the single most reliable indicator of their earnings at age twenty-five.

- Half of the teens and young adults with criminal records or substance abuse problems or both do not read well.
- Among 14- and 15-year-olds who struggle with basic reading and mathematics skills, 20 percent drop out of school within two years.
- A study of fifty-six Georgia and Florida high schools found that schools with extensive transition programs had significantly lower failure and dropout rates than those schools that did not offer comprehensive programs. (Transition Committee: The School District of Greenville County, N.C., 2002)

GETTING A HANDLE ON THE PROBLEM

Every campus principal should have a thumb on the pulse of student success and progress within the school. Keeping a focus on potential problem areas, teacher attitude, school climate, student apathy, and myriad other factors that influence student progress is essential to change the direction of ninth-grade failure. Knowing the students, teachers, and subject areas where the problems exist can contribute greatly to the solutions for changing the pattern of failure at the ninth-grade level. Once the principal has a knowledge base of the problem, it can then be communicated to the appropriate targets; then the empowerment of professional educators begins to have an influence on the direction of the failure rates. Utilizing technology and a student management software package will assist the principal and professional staff in disaggregating the student grade data, enabling one to key in on the problem areas and persistent problems.

STEPS TO PROGRESS

The first step toward doing something about high failure rates in any school is to assess the underlying reasons for the lack of student success. In looking at this problem, one should first access the extant, or existing, databases of definitive data and information available. Once acquired, the data must be broken into every possible component to generate the list of reasons why students seem to be failing. This is known as the quantitative component of the analysis stage of internal research. Some of the common databases to utilize here are grade-reporting-period failure data, attendance-per-grade-reporting period, departmental and teacher breakdowns of per-grade period reports, and teachers' grade books. Any piece of data that might be construed as contributing to a lack of student success should be considered. Other data to consider, of course, are socioeconomic status, family structures, education level of parents, and values of sectors in the community.

The second step in the puzzle is to begin the qualitative or naturalistic process of the quest for success by assessing the staff and teacher perceptions and feelings about why students are experiencing a lack of success. This process can be done on an individual basis or in small-group or team discussions. The questions should be opened and the interviewer should be a nonbiased individual trained in collection of naturalistic data in narrative form. This is the most important and revealing stage of the process. The perceptions of why students are failing on the part of the staff may often be the key to changing the success of many students.

Students should be included in the naturalistic qualitative component of gathering useful data that may contribute to student failure. Student and teacher perceptions of the reasons for failure are often in conflict with one another. Quantitative and qualitative research has shown that teachers' perceptions toward many factors that contribute to students dropping out of school are very different from students' perceptions. In one study, teachers ranked little academic support at home as the number one contributor to students dropping out, while students ranked this same factor as number six on their list (Mireles, 1999). Moreover, students should be surveyed to determine their overall perspective of the factors contributing to failure in school. While quantitative instruments can be effectively utilized to determine the factors that students believe to be associated with failure, additional inquiry by naturalistic means should be employed. A trained interviewer should collect and analyze the narrative data acquired in no less than two rounds of probing in-depth interviews with a sample of students who are purposely selected due to their association with a group of students experiencing failure in the ninth grade. Interviews with students who are experiencing success in school but are in some way connected to groups of students who are not experiencing that same success are also likely candidates for the dialogue and verbal communications component of the research.

Developing a set of relative questions to ask students about why they believe they are failing in the ninth grade can be particularly enlightening. A team of teachers and administrators should draw on experience, rational observation, and, most of all, a review of literature in the process of developing a relevant set of open-ended interview questions.

This stage of the study should not be taken lightly because student responses sometimes get to the root of their perceptions of how teachers teach and how they learn. It is crucial to leave no stone unturned and to dig to the bottom of the barrel in the interview process to find the keys to unlocking the success of students. Often, just becoming aware of the differences and similarities in the research stage fosters a great sense of accomplishment among staff and students; it also serves as a catalyst to allow dialogue between students and teachers about this vitally important topic of student success and lack of success.

Once collected, the data must be analyzed by competent people who can examine and probe quantitative and qualitative data. This may well require the services of one or more consultants with a nonbiased approach to data analysis. Depending on the size of the sample population of students and teachers, there may be a considerable amount of narrative data, which may require a team of qualified data analysts. Computer software is available to do analyses of both quantitative and narrative data. An essential component in this process is completing the analysis and reporting on it in a short period of time to give the parties a sense of ownership and accomplishment in completing as well as participating in the study.

A meaningful side effect of collaboration includes the attribute that students who are working together tend to like school more than in the traditional classroom, which in turn increases student attendance rates. Furthermore, students who like their peers and teachers more are more likely to exhibit altruism and see cooperation as a good thing, which reduces discipline problems in the classroom, thus making teaching more fun and easier for the teacher. This phenomenon alone associated with the collection of data may discourage someone from leaving school. A student may perceive that someone cares as a result of the interviews and surveys and choose to talk with a teacher, administrator, or counselor only to find out they share the same common goal. The process of interviewing and probing for information creates a sense of community as a result of creating dialogue between groups.

DEVELOPING A PLAN OF ACTION

Once these data are analyzed, it is then time to develop the action plan that will turn the failure scenario in a different direction. This process begins with compiling a set of best practices, visiting schools that have been successful in turning the tide, and accessing research-based intervention strategies. Collaboration with a selected group with high stakes and some expertise in student success strategies is a component of success in the development stage. At this stage, sustained incremental staff training is essential to develop the expertise level of the collaborative team of teaching professionals that will carry the torch of change. The way people think will fundamentally require a change. Risk-taking behaviors are a key element in the process of paradigm change, and people will need continuous high-quality motivational training to assist others in the organizational transformation of attitudes and practices.

Developing the plan takes time and high expenditures of energy, but the plan for change must be well thought out and researched. In development of the plan, it is important to look at long-range strategies and avoid the mistake of making too many changes at one time. Two or three major changes or initiatives with follow-up staff development are necessary for successful gains in the reduction of ninth-grade failure. The greatest mistake observed in looking at ninth-grade programs is the attempt to turn the applecart over and start several new interventions with little training. Grounded in staff development research is the basic premise that an effective plan of sustained training and development over a long period of time is critical. The time has come to abandon the common strategy of one-time "shot in the arm" staff development practices of the past and come to the new millennium with a renewed reservoir of ideas that renews and expands teaching professionals over time.

CASES OF FAILURE

In doing research, it was found that the cause of failure is directly related, more than any other factors, to two specific components of student grading: homework grades and test grades. Traditionally, teachers take grades on homework and tests with little regard to other aspects of the learning process. In recent times there has been movement toward more authentic assessment and other modes of assessing student learning. However, in research done with school administrators and teachers in Texas over the last seven years, it is evident that homework and test grades determine the overwhelming majority of ninth graders' success or failure (Marshall, 1995). In light of this finding, some serious work needs to be done to ensure that students are earning sufficient grades in those areas to pass. An array of intervention strategies are available that will alleviate the need for retention in the ninth grade for most students.

Another outcome of the research is that extremely high failure rates in high schools are highly correlated to the organizational attitude that the students are ready for the responsibility of high school when in reality they are not close to that point in their young lives. Assessing administrator, teacher, and staff attitudes and perception will help turn the focus to the real problems associated with student failure.

STUDENT FAILURE OR LACK OF SUCCESS

Research studies over the last decade indicate that the lack of success in school may start at a very early age for many students. Students from areas of high poverty tend to have the greatest obstacles to success, which can be attributed, at least in part, to lack of exposure to the same educational materials and experiences outside their basic environment as their nonpoverty-level counterparts. Students who enter kindergarten from a middle-income home may have been exposed to more than one thousand books by age five (assuming parents could read one book or story a day for five years to their child), whereas a child from an impoverished home may have never experienced any kind of reading material at all. Thus, this creates an unlevel playing field from the beginning, which tends to broaden as time goes on. In these cases, it is the school and the teachers in the organization that must shoulder the burden of creating meaningful educational experiences that promote success. Success breeds success, and positive experiences reassure the child and foster a feeling of pride in accomplishment.

One of the most important aspects of student success is motivation, which is created by climate in the classroom. According to Johnson and Johnson, one of the most important aspects of classroom climate is the students' perceptions of social support, which may be defined as the existence and availability of people on whom one can rely for assistance, support, and caring. Social support is related to performance in achievement situations and is a critical aspect of classroom life (Johnson et al., 1985). In addition, knowing how to access those people and how to engage in meaningful conversations with peers enters as a contributing factor to success. Student success is enhanced when collaborative efforts form. A major difference in students who succeed in school and those who experience difficulty is the level of personal skills acquired through experiences in their life's endeavors. Students who are able and willing to ask for help or work collaboratively in a team are usually more successful in the first years of high school than those who lack these same abilities and skills.

CONCLUSION

After conducting research and observations in schools over the last ten years, a simple yet profound conclusion emerged. Schools must first determine the causes of ninth-grade failure and share them with the professional educational staff as well as other key players within the school system before mounting a quest for change (figure 2.1). A new attitude must be adopted, be disseminated, and prevail for an extended period of time. Involving every stakeholder in the identification of data,

Student Name: _____ DOB:___ /___ /___

Address: _____ Phone:_____

Date/Time Parent Contacted: ___-___-___/___:___ A.M. P.M. By Whom?: _____

Attendance Record: Absences:_____ Tardies:_____

Counseling or other services provided:

_____

_____

_____

Positive Learning Information
List the student's strengths and positive attributes.
1. _____
2. _____
3. _____
4. _____

Teaching and Learning Information
List information and/or factors that limit teaching and learning.
1. _____
2. _____
3. _____
4. _____

Diagnostic and Assessment Information

Reading assessment data	Science assessment data
Math assessment data	Social studies assessment data
Writing assessment data	Other academic assessment data

Other Academic Information
List all other academic information that may contribute to teaching and learning problems.

_____

_____

Figure 2.1. *Ninth-Grade Intervention Team Information Sheet*

Interventions to Date
List all interventions that have been implemented to date, and determine the success level.

Intervention or Teaching Strategy	Describe Level of Success

Recommendations
List recommended strategies and/or interventions to facilitate student success. Include a timeline and evaluation process.

Recommended Interventions or Strategies	Evaluation Process	Timeline

Team Signatures

_____   _____

Figure 2.1.   *(continued)*

contributors, inhibitors, and problems affecting the lives of unsuccessful ninth-grade students is no doubt the beginning of the change process. Finally, developing the plan of action from these data will ensure a higher probability of success for new as well as innovative approaches to modifying the current path of the failure and dropout trend.

REFERENCES

Johnson, D., R. Johnson, L. Buckman, and P. Richards. (1985). The effect of prolonged implementation of cooperative learning on social support with the classroom. *Journal of Psychology* 119(5): 405–411.

Marshall, R. (1995). *The effect of cooperative learning and academic teaming on ninth grade student success in three selected East Texas high schools.* Unpublished dissertation at Texas A&M University–Kingsville, Texas.

Mireles, A. (1999). *Factors associated with student dropouts as perceived by counselors, teachers, and students, in selected South Texas school districts.* Unpublished dissertation at Texas A&M University–Kingsville, Texas.

Transition Committee: The School District of Greenville County, S.C. (2002). Meeting the challenge: The transition to and through ninth grade. Available online at www.greenville.k12.sc.us/district/teachers/trans1.htm [accessed October 3, 2002].

ADDITIONAL WEB RESOURCES

www.csos.jhu.edu/crespar/Reports/report02entire.html#Early%20Evidence. "This site offers early evidence of impact on school climate, attendance, and student promotion."

Maguire, D. "Clusters and Connections: Factors That Contribute to Inuit Dropout." *Capstone Project: Inuit Youth and Dropout Portfolio* (University of Calgary). www.polarnet.ca/~netsilik/Capstone/Visual_site-map.html. "A discussion of the relationships between the various factors follows a visual representation of the factor clusters."

Johnson, R., and D. Johnson. (2002). "Cooperative Learning: Two Heads Learn Better Than One." *In Context: A Quarterly of Human Sustainable Culture.* www.context.org/ICLIB/IC18/Johnson.htm. "This article by Roger and David Johnson concentrates on the three basic ways students can interact with each other as they learn. It elaborates on competitive, individualistic, and cooperative methods of learning. It further explains the process that classrooms must undergo to become more cooperative with less competition as well as individualistic learning."

——. *The Toolroom.* Resource: "Cooperative Learning and Conflict Resolution." www.newhorizons.org/strategies/cooperative/johnson.htm. "This article further explains the components and purposes of cooperative learning in the school environment. It elaborates on the five essential elements to achieve a cooperative learning classroom."

Illinois State Center for the Advancement of Teaching. Collaborative/Cooperative Learning. *Ted's Cooperative Learning and WAC* site (T. Panitz); *Ted's Cooperative Learning E-book* (T. Panitz); "Cooperative Learning Methods: A Meta-Analysis" (D. W. Johnson, R. T. Johnson, and M. B. Stanne). www.cat.ilstu.edu/teaching_tips/collab.shtml. "Illinois State University's Center for the Advancement of Teaching has compiled a set of links for information and assistance in the creation of more collaborative and cooperative learning environments."

Oakes, D. "How to Create a Safe and Healthy School Climate." www.ume.maine.edu/cci/facts/FACTS%202.2/healthysc.html. "In the wake of recent school violence, many educators are asking, How can we improve the climate of schools? How can we create and nurture school environments that are healthy, safe, and inviting? The daunting problems schools face today are, in many ways, symptomatic of the problems plaguing our larger society."

School District of Greenville County Transition Committee. "Meeting the Challenge: The Transition to and through Ninth Grade." www.greenville. k12.sc.us/district/teachers/trans1.htm. "This is a comprehensive transition plan of the School District of Greenville County in South Carolina."

CHAPTER 3

Effective Communications System

In the words of David Thornburg, "I want every classroom in America to be as well equipped as every Coke machine in Japan." Every soft drink machine in Japan has a phone line connected to it so that its automated system can call in orders when its contents reach low levels (Thornburg, 1995). In light of this fact, we have an overwhelming majority of our teachers at the turn of a new century still without the most common basic communications device known to man in the last fifty years. The ability for teachers to communicate with the world outside their classroom via telephone, in most schools, is limited to conference times in noisy workrooms or semiprivate areas, and administrators have little regard for the great benefits or positive impact that such a small device can have on student success, classroom instruction, and classroom management.

COMMUNICATIONS WITH THE HOME

A basic need exists for schools to communicate expectations for students to the home and community in an effective and nonthreatening way. The key factor in changing expectations for student and parent responsibility is effective communications. The school leadership should be compelled to communicate specifically to parents or guardians what is expected of students. An essential element is for teachers, administrators, and staff to develop a system for information dissemination and management that they believe in and buy into wholeheartedly. Myriad telecommunication innovations are making this job easier today than ever before, but the one method that works effectively is contact over the phone on a regular schedule.

Where do I get the telephones? A trend toward support for phones in the classroom is building momentum. This growing support for telecommunications devices in the classroom comes as a result of the safety concerns of many parents and local administrators after some recent disasters and violent behaviors occurred in schools. A twofold benefit comes when teachers are connected to the outside world to communicate with parents, business, industry, and, of course, the main office when the need arises. The E-rate is one valuable source of funding to free up some monies for installation and maintenance of telecommunications systems, but there are many other sources of funds for such ventures. Compensatory funding for at-risk students can be creatively tied to student success, and facilitating communications between parents and teachers is a research-proven method of increasing the success of at-risk population students. Special education and the inclusion of handicapped students in the regular classroom also creates a need for telephone communications not only for safety purposes but also as a benefit to parents, students, and teachers in the effective collaboration of the school and the home. Funding is available, and the innovative leader should seek every means possible to wire classrooms or teacher office spaces or both with telephones and other communications hardware.

AT LEAST TEN PHONE CONTACTS PER WEEK

School leadership should encourage, motivate, or bribe teachers to make at least ten phone contacts per week with parents or guardians. In addition, leaders should develop a system of rewarding teachers who accomplish this task and reduce the failure rate of students as a result of the increased communications with the home. This is a must for successful reduction of failure, which in turn increases student achievement while reducing dropouts. Teachers should be provided with phones in the classroom and time to give feedback to parents. Considerable research has been conducted on telephones in the classroom and the documented effect it has on increasing student success. According to a Texas Center for Educational Technology report, there is overwhelming support by teachers, administrators, and school boards to add phone telecommunications to classrooms (Lucas, 1994).

Teachers are professionals who need the convenience of telecommunications in their classrooms, offices, and lounges. In the business world, professionals have constant access to phones, faxes, and other telecommunications equipment, and educators should be afforded the same. Expect teachers to make regular contact with parents and to include both positive and formative feedback on student work and behavior. We have research available that supports the effectiveness of phones in every classroom. The cost versus the benefit ratio is very small when compared with the cost we incur when a student is retained or takes longer to complete high school or, even worse, drops out of school. School districts that have taken this vital step have seen exceptional results in many aspects of improving school climate, student success, and student achievement as measured by the Texas Assessment of Academic Skills (TAAS). The key element is the campus administrator encouraging and setting the standard for effective use of daily telephone communications and constantly praising, recognizing, and rewarding teachers for the continued successes that come as a result of their efforts.

E-MAIL AND TELECOMMUNICATIONS

As the digital age expands and develops throughout the nation, so does the need to expand the communications capability of the school environment. Teachers, counselors, administrators, and staff can easily extend the communications base with parents through e-mail and other means of telecommunications. We now have the capability to carry out synchronous communications with text, and even video, at only nominal costs to the consumer. The age of digital communications broadens our capabilities with e-mail and web pages to deliver messages to parents or students or both any hour of the day in a user-friendly format that requires less time and effort than traditional phone contact. Free Web access and no-cost Web hosts are available to teachers in a form that allows for easy posting and 24/7 access. Sites such as www.teachers.web.com and teachnet.com as well as other similar Web hosts allow for no-cost communications with all facets of the school community. It is now essential that teachers, administrators, and other school personnel become proficient in Web access and communications capabilities.

The digital age allows the school and community to communicate asynchronously anytime and anywhere, allowing a whole new world to open and expand. It also provides for a learn-anywhere-anytime environment to promote learning like never before. The phenomenal amount of information and knowledge available through telecommunications along with teacher interaction is paving the way to the future. Teachers and administrators who advocate positive communications now have another medium in which positive parental and community relationships can be expanded to further facilitate the transition of ninth-grade students.

WEB COMMUNICATIONS

As the utilization and access to Internet communications continues to flourish throughout the world, so does the need for schools to actively engage in implementing and maintaining a quality website. The site should include vital information useful to parents and patrons of the school. An exemplary site would include weekly activities, teacher sites, school calendar, e-mail addresses of teachers and administrators, phone numbers, emergency information, school safety procedures, as well as important announcements. Teacher sites should include a syllabus or scope and sequence of curriculum, homework assignments, links to help sites, projects, contact information, and most importantly, the teacher's daily schedule with conference times. A well-planned site for the school, staff, and teaching professionals is a key element to improving communications with the home and community.

PARCEL POST COMMUNICATIONS

Many homes are disconnected from any means of telecommunications, and the only method left to communicate with those parents is the

United States Postal System. The regular use of postcards, letters, or other informal methods of written communication is a necessity to involve parents with limited or no access to telephone or Internet communications. Postcards, notes, and letters are also effective with those who have access to telecommunications. The pride that a parent feels in a child can be boosted tremendously by the simplest postcard message from a caring teacher, administrator, or counselor. In addition, the intrinsic motivation that can result from such parental communications is extremely beneficial to the teacher–student and teacher–parent relationship. A simple note — one sentence, or just a big high five on a day's work — goes a long way toward positive relationships and pride of accomplishment.

Teachers and administrators should practice periodic and scheduled communications with parents about topics of interest in and out of the classroom via postal service mail. Progress reports should be mailed, not sent with students, and they should include detailed information about student progress, solutions to problems, as well as positive reinforcement for improvement in performance. Funds should be provided for the purchase of a smiley-face stamp or stickers for all grade levels; this even works with adults. It is amazing how graduate students in their forties and fifties respond to a simple smiley face on their work along with the occasional high-five frog stamp just to let them know that the instructor appreciates their efforts and quality of work. Commitment, enthusiasm, and quality will ensue if the teaching staff and campus leaders set the example for positive reinforcement and communications.

PARENT CONFERENCES

In addition to positive communications, parent–teacher and parent–school relations can be the most effective instrument within the grasp of educators. Indeed, educators should leave no stone unturned in developing constructive interactions with parents. Recruitment and retention of effective communications with the home early in the ninth-grade year can have a lasting effect on support and student success throughout high school. On the other hand, negative relationships will do more to contribute to student failure than we can ever recover. Parents who have a positive relationship with school personnel may tell one or two people, while a parent with a bad experience will tell everyone. Leaders should know the potential problems or challenges and assist in every way possible to minimize the political fallout created from a bad experience.

"Early and often" is a potential motto for a positive communications program aimed at ninth-grade parental involvement. Orientation at the beginning of the year and "getting to know the teacher" meetings are essential. Educators should follow up with early phone calls, e-mail, postcards, and face-to-face conferences during the first few weeks of the ninth-grade experience. Finally, they should replicate this procedure every grade-reporting period and reconvene orientations at the beginning of a new semester. Complacency will be the worst enemy of parental involvement. The old phrase "No news is good news" is not a relevant practice when dealing with ninth-grade students and their parents. Sustaining involvement along with engagement is a monumental task at best.

School leaders should prepare and train teachers well in the process for developing effective conferencing skills. Mentoring this process for new or inexperienced teachers is an absolute necessity to ensure success. The following are just a few things to consider in the development process:

Advance Preparation for Conferences

- *Communicate your concerns early:* Make your first contact with parents the first week of school, communicating the positive attributes you are observing. Catch the child doing things right and tell the child and the parents. When problems arise, notify parents early and document potential concerns as they arise.
- *Document challenges:* Record accurate accounts of discipline and behavior incidents. Prepare printouts of grades and progress toward assigned works. Maintain a record of all communications with parents. Keep a diary of specific problems that may be influencing progress.
- *Utilize support personnel:* Develop rapport and positive relationships with school counselors, psychologists, special education

staff, and other professionals who have particular expertise in specialized areas or concern. Enlisting the assistance of support personnel is a professional attribute, not a sign of weakness or lack of knowledge.

Effective Conferencing

- *Do the homework:* Collaborate with campus leaders, support personnel, and teaching colleagues who have experienced conferences with the parents or student or both in the past. Prepare data and information prior to contact with the parents.
- *Meeting and greeting parents:* Prepare for specialized meetings, and greet the parents in a cordial, professional manner. Seek the assistance of colleagues and support staff to determine if special accommodations may be needed, such as translators or special needs for a handicapping condition. Begin and end the conference with something especially positive about the student.
- *Documentation and minutes:* No meeting is complete without the paperwork. Keep accurate minutes or recordings of the proceeding of the meeting. Complete a follow-up report, and send copies of the meeting record to all attendees.
- *Select words carefully:* Keep a calm, relaxed tone and select your words carefully. Parents may construe criticisms as an accusation of inappropriate parenting. Stay calm, cool, and collected.
- *Listen:* You were given two ears and one mouth, and perhaps there is a message within the human anatomy. Listen carefully, and allow the parent to express anger and discontent. Note all concerns, and then work through each of the concerns. Listen first, note the concern, and then collaborate with a solution.

TRAINING

One of the most important factors for educators to remember is that parents have differing levels of skills and comfort zones when it comes to school involvement and helping motivate their children. In light of the differences, it is important to train teachers in effective communications and conferencing skills. Sustained staff development over an extended period of time, which refines and emphasizes quality communications skills, both written and verbal, is essential for success in the implementation and maintenance of a school community-relations program. "A checklist" for effective communications and conferencing skills as well as prepared forms for conferencing can be found in the proceding figures (see figures 3.1–3.3).

A. Advanced Preparation
- ☐ Ensure that the meeting room is clean and comfortable
- ☐ Determine need for resource personnel or facilitators
- ☐ Confirm that conference announcement has been sent and received
- ☐ Make certain all possible supplies are readily available and organized
- ☐ Secure a collection of diverse reading materials for guests
- ☐ Make sure an attractive and motivational setting is available for young children
- ☐ Conference participants are aware of messages sent by body language

B. Facilities/Documents
- ☐ Provide a timeline up front for the conference
- ☐ Secure all needed furniture, tables, and equipment
- ☐ Make sure documents are prepared and ready for the conference participants
- ☐ Have a special area with toys or other items available for toddlers

C. Enhancing Conference Communications
- ☐ Comments related to the positive attributes of the child come first
- ☐ A quality account or summary of student works is prepared and provided
- ☐ Student works are organized and sequenced for the conference
- ☐ Evidence is based on facts and adequate justification is presented
- ☐ All participants are encouraged to provide input and solutions
- ☐ Questions are answered in layman's terminology
- ☐ Unanswered questions are documented
- ☐ Answers to unanswered questions are provided promptly in a follow-up letter
- ☐ A verbal summary is made by the conference leader
- ☐ The conference closes with other positive attributes of the child and parent
- ☐ Sincere appreciation is expressed for participants' time and effort
- ☐ A written summary is provided in a timely manner

D. Closing the Meeting
- ☐ Develop a collaborative and unified plan of action
- ☐ Develop a time frame and monitoring procedure for teachers and parents
- ☐ Follow up the conference with a telephone call within a few days
- ☐ Enlist the support and participation of parents for future assistance
- ☐ Emphasize the high priority of conference confidentiality
- ☐ Document parent conference results with signed documents
- ☐ Maintain a file for every parent conference in more than one place

---

Figure 3.1. *Checklist for Effective Conferencing*

Teacher name: _____

Student: _____

Contact: _____

Phone numbers: _____

Date/Time:_____

Topics to be discussed: _____
_____
_____
_____
_____
_____

Priorities: _____ Successful

_____ Yes _____ No

_____ Yes _____ No

_____ Yes _____ No

_____ Yes _____ No

_____ Yes _____ No

_____ Yes _____ No

_____ Yes _____ No

Figure 3.2.   *Telephone Conversation Plan*

Opportunities and modes of communication have never been more plentiful than in the age of information. We can e-mail, instant message, chat, and even desktop videoconference from the comfort of our home or office. Communications can be synchronous or asynchronous, and if all else fails, we still have the telephone and United States Postal Service as a means of building relationships with parents and community. Never before have we had so much ability to communicate, and school leaders should be on the forefront of initiating positive communications between teachers and parents. Exemplary leaders facilitate quality relationships between the school and the community. All the tools for developing the

The major task in many parent conferences is simply breaking the ice and opening the lines of communication between participants. The list below offers ideas and prompts for beginning this very important process on a positive stroke:

Hello, _____, (know the name of the parent before arrival) I am _____ (provide your name and position). I want to thank you for taking time out of your day to visit with us today about _____ (student's name) and his/her progress in school.

Our education team would like to provide you with a sketch and documents about _____, (student's name) progress this grading period. Confidentiality will be a very high priority, and copies of all documents will be made available only to you, the parent.

Before we begin, I would like to tell you how much we appreciate the opportunity to share the positive things we have found about _____ (student's name).

Next, we would like to discuss _____ (student's name) progress in school. (At this point, provide the highly organized documents of the progress or lack of progress.)

_____ (student's name) behavior has been _____, and we find it important to share the concerns or positive comments. (Provide factual evidence of positive and/or negative behavior incidents.)

We ask that you help us design an intervention plan to assist with _____ (student's name) success in school. Your input and ideas are most welcome here. The team looks forward to working with you to create positive solutions. (Create timelines and specific goals for improvement while listening carefully to the parent.)

Let us summarize what we have discussed. _____ (student's name) will be working on the following things at home to improve his/her success in school. These are things we discussed as possible strategies, and these are our defined goals. Are there any we might add or delete from the summary? (Provide copies of the proceeding of the meeting in writing ASAP.)

Here is my business card and our team contact information. You will find our e-mail addresses, conference times, and home and school phone numbers for your convenience. Feel free to contact us with concerns or positive things you might have to share.

We would like to thank you again for taking the time to become a part of our student success team. We look forward to a great working relationship with you to ensure _____ (student's name) success in school.

Figure 3.3. Team Conference Script for Beginners

communicative bonds that foster student success and achievement are awaiting the futuristic and visionary campus leader.

CONCLUSION

Next to quality instruction, one of the most beneficial tasks that administrators and teachers can perform is regular and effective communications with the home. It takes time and commitment; however, the rewards or gains reaped from this effort are invaluable. The more parents are informed of student progress or involved in educational interventions, the more we can expect improvement in success as well as achievement. Every parent will not respond in a positive manner; nonetheless, efforts to connect school and home environments yield significant benefits. Past experiences and research indicate a strong correlation between teacher–parent collaboration and increases in student success at all levels in the educational process. A strong, regimented communications plan, with commitment from all stakeholders, is an essential link in the chain of school improvements. Encouraging continuous collaboration among administrators, teachers, and parents/guardians is, without a doubt, well worth the time expended.

REFERENCES

Lucas, L. (1994). Telephones in the classroom. Texas Computer Educators Association (TCEA). Paper presented at the annual TCEA conference, Austin, Tex.

Thornburg, D. (1995). Personal interview by author. February.

ADDITIONAL WEB RESOURCES

Prentice Hall, Professional Development Web page. "Communications Checklist." www.phschool.com/professional_development/teaching_tools/teaching_ to_the_middle/middle_grades_experience/communications_checklist.cfm. "Open and frequent communication is a key to effective family involvement in the schools. Use this checklist to make sure that you are using all the communication channels that are available to you."

"Communications." *Groveland Elementary School Parent Handbook*. www.minetonka.k12.mn.us/groveland/handbook/communications.html. "Groveland Elementary School in Minnetonka, Minnesota, has posted their parent handbook at this location, and it includes a critical section on communication between the school and the parents."

"School Parent Communications: Parental Involvement." *Burnside State High School*. www.burnsideshs.qld.edu.au/school-parent_communications.htm. "The Burnside State High School website has great examples of parent communications and delineates how parents can communicate with the school. The site also has links to newsletters, concerns and worries, special events, and reporting."

University of Illinois Extension. "Parent/Teacher Communications and Establishing a Relationship with Your Child's Teacher." *Urban Programs Resource Network*. www.urbanext.uiuc.edu/familyworks/school-01.html. "This site offers tips for creating positive parent–teacher relationships. The most positive communication a parent can have with a teacher is communication that says, 'I care about my child, and I value school.' The best way a parent can show how much he or she values learning is by sending a prepared child to school every day. When a child is absent from school, important lessons may be missed. Once a child gets behind in class, catching up can be difficult."

Center for Applied Special Technology (CAST). "The Role of Online Communications in Schools: A National Study." *CAST Universal Design for Learning*. www.cast.org/udl/index.cfm?i=121. "This article demonstrates that students with online access perform better."

Northwest Regional Educational Laboratory. "Parent Volunteers: Good for Students and Schools." www.nwrel.org/nwreport/aug99/article9.html. "Northwest Regional Educational Laboratory maintains this site to help schools develop parent relations. The site includes a link to Parent Partners: Using Parents to Enhance Education."

"Creating a Positive Climate: Parent Involvement." *Safe and Responsive Schools Project*. www.indiana.edu/~safeschl/ParentInvolvement.pdf. "This website is a result of the Safe and Responsive Schools Project, which is funded by a three-year grant from the U.S. Department of Education, Office of Special Education Programs, and is dedicated to developing and studying prevention-based approaches to school safety."

National Campaign for Public School Improvement. "A Checklist for an Effective Parent–School Partnership." *Project Appleseed*. www.projectappleseed.org/chklst.html. Project Appleseed has developed and posted "A Checklist for an Effective Parent–School Partnership." "Joyce Epstein of Johns Hopkins University postulates that one way to start improving your school's parent–school partnerships is by assessing present practices."

Long Beach (N.Y.) Classroom Teachers Association. "Ten Things You Should Never Do at a Parent Conference." www.nysut.org/longbeach/Tenthings.html. "This site is a must-see site, particularly for new teachers. It is a compilation of a great list of pitfalls teachers could fall into in a good-faith effort to improve communications with parents. *New York Teacher* interviewed experienced classroom teachers, including master teachers who offer courses in the union's Effective Teaching Program. Discussed are their thoughts on ten common mistakes, along with ways to have a successful session."

Indiana University, South Bend, Families and Education Network. "Practical Tips for Improving Parent–Teacher Communication." www.iuinfo.indiana.edu/ocm/packages/parnteac.htm. "One sure trigger of the primal 'fight or flight' response is getting a phone call that begins, 'This is Susie's teacher' or 'This is Johnnie's parent.' Those words can revive childhood memories of unpleasant trips to the principal's office, resulting in a negative effect on parent–teacher communication."

Teachnet.Com. "Weekly Parent Activity." www.teachnet.com/how-to/pr/index.html. "This school is installing a Parent–Teacher Hotline, a telephone system that allows teachers to record messages to their parents; parents can call in, enter the classroom ID number and hear the teacher's message regarding homework, upcoming activities, permission slips that need to be returned, and so forth. We will be using ours to include a Home Activity for the Week, a simple learning activity designed to involve parents in the learning/teaching process."

———. "Creating a Classroom Newsletter." www.teachnet.com/how-to/pr/newsltr.html. "By keeping the process simple you will not feel completely overwhelmed, and your newsletter will more likely go out on a timely basis. Creating a work of art may sound nice, but the first priority is getting the news out."

Teaching.Com. www.teaching.com/ttalk/.com "'Teacher Talk' is a discussion forum where K–12 teachers can discuss teaching techniques, trade lesson plan ideas, and support one another."

Community Communications. "The Teacher's Lounge." www.comcom121.org/tlounge/. "A free tutorial for a teacher who has a failing student. Includes free coaching in a private forum."

Family Education Network. "Teacher-Parent Collaboration." www.teachervision.com/lesson-plans/lesson-3730.html. "This site provides a superior set of forms and resources for effective parent conferences. In addition to parent conference forms, the site provides other resources to distribute to parents related to help for homework and reports."

CHAPTER 4

Putting Brakes on Failure Rates

For ten or more years, high schools have tried to ease the transition to high school and boost ninth-grade performance. They have adjusted schedules to give students more chances to earn credits. They have developed individualized programs to help students catch up. They have even created a separate wing at some high schools and entire campuses devoted only to ninth graders so that school will be less overwhelming for them, The results of these efforts are mixed. Statewide, the percentage of students failing ninth grade has not improved significantly in over five years. In addition, four out of five students who drop out do so in part because they are older than their peers (Kurtz, 1999).

Administrators and teachers are faced with major decisions centered around the problems of ninth-grade failure. What can be done and how fast can a school get the situation under control? Doing nothing will not make the problem just go away. Taking the bull by the horns so the brakes can be applied to stop the cycle is the essential decision at hand. It is well known that when you are up to your ears in alligators, it is difficult to remember that the main objective was to drain the swamp, but getting the foot on the brake to stop failure is a good place to start.

Educating parents is a monumental task at best in the two-income family or single-parent households that dominate our society and school communities. However, it is essential to communicate the paramount importance of parental involvement and verbal engagement with teenagers. Ninth graders can succeed in making it through the freshman experience if parents are educated to do the following:

- Ask the child how he or she is doing in school regularly.
- Maintain contact with teachers on a consistent schedule.
- Listen to the teen with open friendly conversation.
- Visit the high-school facility with the student at the beginning of the year.
- Show the teen that you are interested in his or her education.
- Persist in the quest for a quality education.

The importance of being involved is unsurpassed by any other responsibility as a parent. High-school students are not likely to say they want parents involved, but deep inside their souls, they want parents to care and exhibit a sincere concern about their education. The role of the administrators and teachers is to communicate the importance of involvement to parents and do everything within their power to initiate as well as maintain a high level of parental engagement through activities that foster the school/parent/student relationship.

Early on, schools need to sponsor an orientation for ninth graders and their parents. If resources are available, an evening meal to attract busy parents and community members usually facilitates attendance while building a positive relationship. When the school provides a relatively low-cost meal and communicates the importance of parental involvement, the majority of parents will make an effort to come. If attendance is not satisfactory, the school should try again and again until parents are fully involved.

Well-planned and organized orientations that do not waste the time and effort of parents serve as a catalyst for positive communications and build vital trust relationships between school and home. A poorly organized meeting will do great damage to parental involvement and participation. Be mindful that parents' lives are busy and that a sequence of events in an orderly environment is desirable. Seeing all sides of the school environment from the perspective of a teacher, administrator, and a nine-time parent has helped me understand the importance of organization and structure to meetings or school events. One can destroy more positive relations in a one-hour meeting without focus than can be built in a decade. With this in mind, educators should carefully plan, rehearse, and organize every event where parents and community members are present in the school.

CONNECTION WITH A CARING ADULT

Foremost, the student in transition needs connection with a caring adult both at school and at home. In many instances, the absence of the caring adult at home cannot be shouldered by the school system. A child's relationship with a caring teacher who is willing to do whatever it takes to ensure that students are successful in their classes and with others as well cannot be stressed enough. The ninth grade is a pivotal year in a student's life, and the support group or team of teaching professionals created by the school during this transition year is crucial to the success of the students. Research on transition programs has proven that a few intervention strategies can go a long way toward keeping children in school and reducing the huge aforementioned numbers of children who are not completing high school. The key ingredient to that transition is creating a driving force of teacher attitudes that student success is our business. A group of academic teachers who persistently choose to care about a specific group of kids breeds the future success of those individuals. We must engrain in the students the same drive required to complete a college degree and the same commitment it takes to pass a driver's exam. Educators need to find the motivation within the child to succeed.

One of the highest compliments ever given to an educator that I can remember is when a group of children were asked to write something about their favorite teacher. One child wrote, "Mrs. Chandler is a great teacher because she made me get up off my lazy butt and read." This is the kind of teacher that every child wants but often does not have. Mrs. Chandler was more persistent than the child and required him, through whatever means necessary, to become successful in reading. She was the caring adult who took the responsibility for the child's success. What does success mean? Success is seeing the light come on and students extending themselves and reaching for more. Moreover, success will be seen when large numbers of ninth-grade students are no longer retained and move on to experience subsequent success in high school because a caring team of teachers, administrators, counselors, and parents took the time and effort to persist to the end.

EMPOWERING THE TEACHERS

A campus leader can only do so much to influence success; it is the teaching professionals who are closest to the problem that will ultimately make the impact on ninth-grade failure rates. Teachers should receive professional development, motivation and encouragement, as well as support from administration in the transition period and beyond. A well-researched and critical practice that can influence student success is reduction of the student-to-teacher ratio. If a school system can only implement one practice to influence failure, reduction of class size is the most important. In problem areas such as math, science, and English, a student-to-teacher ratio of ten students per class would be the most desirable. Financial constraints may hamper such efforts, however. In these instances, innovative thinking and creative scheduling are the keys to making the necessary changes to reduce the student-to-teacher ratio where success becomes a common practice.

Providing teachers and other educational professionals with the tools to facilitate success becomes more important as the process is set in motion. Teachers need regularly scheduled events for team meetings and access to telecommunications equipment such as phones, fax machines, copiers, and e-mail. Principals need to be mindful of needs and provide the tools for building effective relationships with students, parents, and the community prior to implementation of an improvement process.

Empowerment will come if the campus leader provides the support, inspiration, and motivation for continuous sustained improvement of ninth-grade success initiatives. Utilizations of the correct situational leadership components appropriate for the individuals and groups at the proper stages of development will maintain the direction and continuity needed for growth and improvement for students. Eventually, group dynamics should reach a stage of total autonomy, and the campus principal simply gets paid for watching the successes that the empowered groups turn out on a daily basis. Yes, this is the pie in the sky, but with empowerment, professional development, and support of the leader, it usually happens.

TIME AND TOOLS FOR SUCCESS

Time to communicate with grade-level team members and parents is a highly significant factor contributing to success of students. Teachers must be provided with the time to collaborate and, then, communicate concerns and triumphs to parents and other caring adults connected with students. Again, creative scheduling and innovative thinking are the keys to finding the time within or outside the school day for a meaningful program aimed at increasing the levels of teacher-to-home communications. Whether it is sending notes, e-mail, or phone communications, time is of utmost importance to connect the caring adults, teachers, and parents in a meaningful dialogue to improve student support systems.

Alone, time will not provide the impetus to motivate teachers to communicate. Training in effective communication with parents along with a connection to experienced teaching professionals who possess skills in this area are a prescription for success. New teachers need assistance with their first conferences and should be teamed with experienced professionals with a plethora of skills in leading conferences and parental communications. Effective communications go a long way in improving relationships with students, parents, and the community. When educators begin to initiate a program to improve communications, they should remember that it is the parents' money and their children's future that are at stake.

In addition to time, an environment for effective professional meetings between parents and/or students and professional educators enhances the probability of success in building meaningful relationships. User-friendly offices or conferencing facilities with a positive tone can go a long way in helping set the stage for good interaction and dialogue between the interested parties. Many parents have small children with them during conferences, and a place within the conference room for children to play and stay occupied is an excellent idea to promote effective conferencing. A small corner with safe toys, books, and possibly a teacher's aide to super-vise the small children during the conference makes the meeting with par-ents go more smoothly with minimal interruption. A number of schools have day-care facilities incorporated within the school facility, and send-ing small children to these facilities during a conference further supports the notion that the school is a place where parents are welcome and col-laboration is a part of ensuring student success.

Teaching professionals need advance preparation and materials for building the communications bridge. A collection of books, websites, forms, and handbooks are helpful tools that can be developed over time to create the foundation for a quality-improvement program. School leaders should assist in the development of forms for documenting calls, confer-ences, and parent visits. Forms such as a checklist for pre-conference preparation, documentation, grade-improvement contracts, and home-work agreements are sometimes effective tools for developing commit-ment. One of the most intriguing pieces of paperwork acquired from cam-pus visits has been a parent–teacher and student–teacher consensus agreement, which is developed during a conference by a third party to es-tablish an obligation toward improvement and assurances from all parties.

MOTIVATION

School leaders can foster student motivation by creating a positive school culture; student motivation can be generated by using activities, statements of goals, behavior codes, rituals, and symbols and messages (Renchler, 1992). The expectations and attitudes toward education can be shaped by the school's culture; school leaders who effectively man-age this aspect can boost student and teacher motivation, thus impact-ing their learning (Renchler, 1992). Renchler believes that the optimum school climate is created by

- stressing goal setting and self-regulation/management
- offering students choices
- rewarding students for achieving personal-best goals
- developing teamwork through group learning and problem-solving experiences

- moving from a testing culture to an assessment culture (self-assessment and authentic evaluation)
- teaching time-management skills and offering self-paced instruction

In the analysis of school cultures, it has been found that the culture of an organization contributes greatly to exemplary performance. In addition, school cultures that are strong, positive, and collaborative tend to encourage and reward the professionals' ongoing task of organizational improvement (Deal, 1993).

Research seems to suggest that the motivation level of the leader influences the motivation of teachers, which subsequently impacts the motivation level of students. In the process of visiting numerous campuses over time, a conclusion has been drawn from observation that the school usually takes on the personality of its leader(s). It follows that teachers and students exemplify the motivation and energy levels of the administrator or the strong informal leadership. Therefore, the motivational climate within the confines of a school and the daily reinforcement of teachers as well as the students rests solely on the broad shoulders of a dynamic leader. It is a heavy load!

STAYING ON THE BRAKES

Once the brakes have been applied, staying on the pedal and keeping a steady application to end the upward movement of failure rates is an exhausting task. Like the brakes in an automobile, when applied continuously, friction causes heat and excessive wear on the components of the braking system. A team of individuals riding the brakes on failure will need renewal and positive reinforcement from their administrators. Diagnosing the levels of stress, looking for signs of fatigue, and/or the symptoms of burnout are crucial in trying to keep the team members cool and functioning to the end of the journey. The effective administrator will always be in the diagnostic mode, providing needed renewal activities such as social gatherings, stress-relief sessions, or special praise for the small incremental successes along the way to sustain the staff motivation necessary for improvement (figure 4.1).

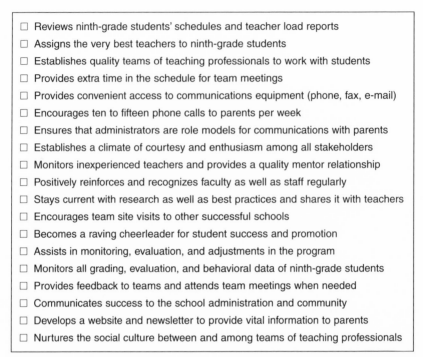

Figure 4.1. *Applying the Brakes to the Failure Mobile Principal's Responsibilities Checklist*

REFERENCES

Deal, T. E. (1993). The culture of schools. In *Educational leadership and school culture,* edited by M. Sashkin and H. J. Walberg. Berkeley, Calif.: McCutchan.

Kurtz, M. (1999). Schools, teens battle barrier of ninth grade. *Austin American-Statesman,* May 23, 1999.

Renchler, R. (1992). School leadership and student motivation. *ERIC Digest* 71 [online], ED346558. Eugene, Oreg.: ERIC Clearinghouse on Educational Management.

ADDITIONAL WEB RESOURCES

Terry, P. M. (2001). "Empowering Teachers as Leaders." *National FORUM Journals* 11E(3). www.nationalforum.com/TERRYte8e3.html. "This article presents the need for what some view as a rather radical change in educational leadership. An argument for this change is proffered by reviewing the current leadership methodology and, for comparison, empowerment is explored as it relates to teacher leadership."

Maguire, D. "School Leaders." *Capstone Project: Inuit Youth and Dropout Portfolio* (University of Calgary). www.polarnet.ca/~netsilik/Capstone/School_Leader2.html. "Teacher motivation is an important factor in creating student success; this article keys in on the connection between teacher motivation and student success in school."

———. Review of "School Leadership and Student Motivation," by Ron Renchler. *Capstone Project: Inuit Youth and Dropout Portfolio* (University of Calgary). www.polarnet.ca/~netsilik/Capstone/AR-Renchler.html. "This article offers six policies and programs that can influence a positive environment. Renchler believes that the optimum school climate is created by the six policies and programs listed and explained in the article."

Metler, C. M. "The Teacher Motivation and Job Satisfaction Survey." personal.bgsu.edu/~mertler/TMJS-Survey/TMJS.html. "This online survey could be beneficial in assessing what motivates your teachers and/or teams of teachers."

"Improving Student Motivation Survey." www.serve.org/assessment/accountability/TeacherSurvey.doc. "The purpose of this survey is to explore teachers' perceptions of factors that affect student motivation."

"Teacher Motivation and Capabilities." *School Improvement in Maryland.* www.mdk12.org/practices/benchmark/improve/study/phaseone/esss-2.html. "This site offers a study of higher success and lower success elementary schools."

Renchler, R. (1992). "School Leadership and Student Motivation." *ERIC Digest* 71, ED346558. www.ed.gov/databases/ERIC_Digests/ed346558.html. "This *ERIC Digest* article focuses on the fact that making the classroom a place that naturally motivates students to learn is much easier when students and teachers function in an atmosphere where academic success and the motivation to learn are expected and rewarded."

"Motivation in the Classroom." www.indiana.edu/~eric_rec/ieo/bibs/mot-gen.html. "The materials at this site should assist teachers in creating motivation in the classroom. The site contains some general theories and classroom strategies and practices."

Academic Learning Services, University of Oregon. *Teaching Effectiveness Program.* tep.uoregon.edu/resources/index.html. "The Teaching Effectiveness Program at the University of Oregon provides a wide range and variety of valuable resources for instructors."

A to Z Teacher Stuff Network. "Tips: Motivating Students." www. atozteacherstuff.com/tips/Motivating_Students. "This website offers teacher-created tips for motivating students. It allows for additional responses from practitioners on the topic of motivation in the classroom. The site also offers a forum for communications among teaching professionals and others to facilitate higher levels of student motivation."

CHAPTER 5

Developing the TEAM

Perceivably, developing the team concept could be one of the most daunting tasks of all in the quest to increase student success in schools. Removing the barriers of time and constraints of policy can cause even the most creative to feel stress. The instructional time requirements, the duty-free lunch period, as well as the limits placed on teacher conferences, must be considered in developing a master schedule that supports the structure of teaming. One thought always comes back when reflecting on finding time for teaming. How do schools find time for a pep rally or an assembly and yet make excuses for why they cannot find time for the most important part of a school day—teaming time for teachers, counselors, parents, administrators, and students?

TEAMS DEFINED

Teams are people working together for a shared vision, measurable goal, or purpose. Members of the team exchange views and dialogue about problems, explore information, formulate solutions, and collaborate with others. They arrive at a consensus with team support of plans for implementation. The team's success is solely based on progress toward a specified goal. On an educational level, all members are jointly responsible for accomplishments, victories, disappointments, and failures. According to Bateman (1990), quality teams possess the following characteristics:

- High level of interdependence among team members.
- Team leader has good people skills and is committed to team approach.

- Each team member is willing to contribute.
- Members develop a relaxed climate for communication.
- Members develop a mutual trust.
- Team and individuals are prepared to take risks.
- Team has clear goals and established targets.
- Each member's role is defined.
- Members know how to examine team and individual errors without attacks.
- Members possess the capacity to create new and innovative ideas.
- Each team member knows he or she can influence the team agenda.

IMPLEMENT A SYSTEM OF INTERDISCIPLINARY TEAMING

Development of the team concept among teaching and paraprofessional staff is invaluable in increasing the success of the students they serve. Everyone from the custodian, to the teacher's aide, to the office secretarial staff should be involved with the teaching team to guarantee the success of every child within the school. Incorporate teachers, counselors, administrators, and staff as case managers for all students, and provide time for teachers to connect with students on a regular basis. If a school leader can only do one thing, teaming is the key to making the first step toward decreasing failure, increasing scores on tests for academic skills, and increasing graduation rates.

SIGNIFICANCE OF ACADEMIC TEAMING

Academic teams or teacher-assistance teams, as they are sometimes referred to, are among the viable interventions or alternative programs that can be implemented to address many of the needs of the students currently enrolled in public schools. Academic teams can support the collaboration and empowerment of teachers, address student and school-wide problems, provide preventive intervention for at-risk students, and identify appropriate referrals to special services inside and outside the school setting (Chalfant et al., 1991). These teams of teachers, when provided with proper training, become a school-based problem-solving unit to assist students with particular problems that inhibit their success in or out of school (figure 5.1). The academic team of teachers concept

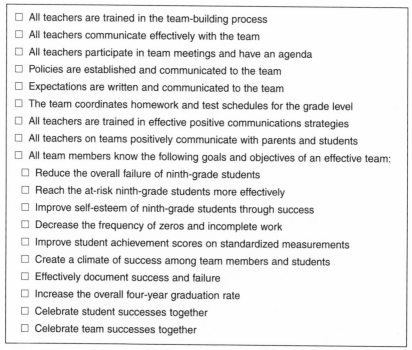

☐ All teachers are trained in the team-building process
☐ All teachers communicate effectively with the team
☐ All teachers participate in team meetings and have an agenda
☐ Policies are established and communicated to the team
☐ Expectations are written and communicated to the team
☐ The team coordinates homework and test schedules for the grade level
☐ All teachers are trained in effective positive communications strategies
☐ All teachers on teams positively communicate with parents and students
☐ All team members know the following goals and objectives of an effective team:
  ☐ Reduce the overall failure of ninth-grade students
  ☐ Reach the at-risk ninth-grade students more effectively
  ☐ Improve self-esteem of ninth-grade students through success
  ☐ Decrease the frequency of zeros and incomplete work
  ☐ Improve student achievement scores on standardized measurements
  ☐ Create a climate of success among team members and students
  ☐ Effectively document success and failure
  ☐ Increase the overall four-year graduation rate
  ☐ Celebrate student successes together
  ☐ Celebrate team successes together

Figure 5.1. *Teacher Team Checklist*

provides a format in which classroom instructors can meet on a timely basis to devise solutions cooperatively that inherently assist students directly or indirectly to succeed in their educational endeavors. Incorporating academic teams into schools may help students and other teachers understand classroom problems and generate solution strategies to solve particular problems. Academic teams in many schools also serve as interdisciplinary teams to integrate curriculum and generate classroom methods whereby thematic lessons enhance student success. The basic premise is that academic teams exist to support the educational environment for both teachers and students to deal with the wide variety of issues that are encountered in the educational process.

ACADEMIC TEAMING BACKGROUND

As many as 25 percent of the students in American classrooms experience difficulties with school; furthermore, many students are unsuccessful in completing the rigors of high-school requirements for graduation.

The public schools of this time are under extreme scrutiny to meet the needs of children and prepare them to be lifelong learners. To accomplish this task, the educational system must change or transform from preparing students in the traditional ways of the past to embarking on new and innovative ways to address the needs of the student population of the current generation. Today's schoolchildren have more than educational needs; an ever-increasing number of children face myriad problems outside the classroom, which have a devastating impact on their ability to learn. The need for a viable school intervention team to ease the frustrations and problems that face today's youth cannot be overemphasized in order to facilitate success in the classroom.

In current field practice, educators move students through the educational system with little regard to individual needs, which facilitates failure for far too many students. An intervention program, referenced in literature and practiced as academic teams, attempts to circumvent this paradigm and change the way educators deal with students (Oches, 1989). The major purpose of these teams is to break the cycle of student failure by focusing on problems within the educational system and personalizing student-related problems. The academic teams are responsible for the individual success groups of students, and their major function is to attempt to identify problems within the system that are in conflict with student needs.

THE FUNCTION OF ACADEMIC TEAMS

Academic teams of teachers are teacher oriented, and composed primarily of classroom teachers. They function as a general educational consultation alternative and serve as an avenue for empowerment of the classroom teaching element of a school (Chalfant and Van Dusen Pysh, 1989).

Some of the activities of academic teams are listed below (Mac Iver and Epstein, 1991):

- Consult with students about particular problems.
- Discuss social relations with other students.
- Discuss personal or family problems.

- Discuss health issues such as drug-use prevention, family planning, and so forth.
- Discuss moral or ethical issues/values.
- Discuss intergroup relations and multicultural issues.
- Discuss academic problems.
- Discuss self-confidence and leadership issues.
- Provide counseling and information on careers.
- Provide information on postsecondary education.
- Provide instructional support and intervention strategies for other teachers.
- Integrate lessons for thematic teaching.

RESEARCH AND IMPLEMENTATION

Academic teaming, a particularly interesting phenomenon, is best characterized by the following quote: "Teachers ordinarily have few forums to share their problems in a professional way and brainstorm solutions with one another. Building-level teams provide a forum where teachers, like physicians, can consult with one another, share their expertise, and benefit from one another's experience and areas of speciality" (Chalfant et al., 1991). In addition, this quote can be expanded to include students who have had very few opportunities in the traditional school system to share ideas and problems with trained, caring professionals who have the ability to help solve the problems that inhibit their potential success in the educational process. The school-based academic teacher team is a concerted effort to assist students and teachers with a more effective way to solve the problems related to learning as well as behavioral problems within the general classroom setting.

In Arkansas, a three-step plan of action was initiated in 1991 when Dr. Margaret Van Dusen Pysh and Dr. James Chalfant were invited to speak to the Arkansas Department of Education about the implications and benefits of establishing their Teacher Assistance Team Model in Arkansas schools. The Arkansas Department of Education, as a result of the presentation, determined that the presence of such teams offered several potential benefits to the educational system, including the following: providing a support system for teachers; serving as a preventive measure for at-risk students and assisting in mainstreaming special education students; addressing problems in schools; enhancing teachers' effectiveness through new perceptions, skills, and behaviors; enhancing teacher morale; producing changes in teachers' interpersonal behaviors; and reducing referral rates and cost (Chalfant et al., 1991). In this process, seven phases were carried out beginning with planning and then extending through a process of developing support, training, implementation, follow-up training, advanced training, and evaluation. The results of the Arkansas program reinforce previous research showing that academic teams can support and enhance the collaboration and empowerment of teachers, address student and schoolwide problems, provide preventive intervention for at-risk students, and identify appropriate referrals to special education (Chalfant et al., 1991).

The keys to effective implementation of such a program rest on the commitment of the staff and support from the administration of the school system, with the most critical factor being the campus principal's support for the process of implementation. The commitment to the academic teaming process must be long term and involve ongoing training and evaluation, with the fortitude to adjust the implementation process based on the annual evaluation of the program.

As for the particular mechanics of the implementation of the academic teaming concept, the key elements to potential success of the intervention are time for the staff to interact and allowances for the teams to have common planning periods. This takes a great deal of commitment from administration in allocation of time, staffing, and finances. According to research, 36 percent of the schools that use interdisciplinary academic teams give team members two or more hours of common planning time each week, and less than 60 percent of all teams have a formal team leader (Mac Iver and Epstein, 1991). The results of such research suggest that to realize the benefits of a responsive practice, schools must make sure that the practices are implemented properly. The academic teaming process will yield few benefits unless the teachers actually use the time to provide frequent social and emotional support activities to students (Mac Iver and Epstein, 1991). This further establishes the need for extensive training and staff development activities in advance of implementation of an academic teaming intervention program.

CONCLUSION

Team building raises the possibility that education might be improved by the formation of a nucleus of committed people in each school, people prepared to take risks inside and outside the classrooms (Maeroff, 1993). The concept and process of team building also follows the current trends in business and industry, which further strengthens the argument for changing the paradigm of education to emulate and facilitate the transition from school to work. The teaming concept serves as a medium to increase efficiency, effectiveness, and motivation in our schools, and ultimately in the place of employment for all students. Developing effective teams of educators may be one of the most overwhelming tasks for the effective leader; however, the benefits of enduring the pain brought on by group dynamics have proven to be extremely rewarding to the educational organizations' climate while positively influencing student success toward graduation.

REFERENCES

Bateman, A. (June 1990). Team building: Developing a productive team. Lincoln: Nebraska Cooperative Extension CC352. Available online at www.ianr.unl.edu/pubs/Misc/cc352.htm [accessed October 10, 2002].

Chalfant, J., and M. Van Dusen Pysh. (1989). Teacher assistance teams: Five descriptive studies on 96 teams. *Remedial and Special Education (RASE)* 10(6): 49–58.

Chalfant, J., et al. (1991). Teacher assistance teams: Supporting at-risk students in rural areas. A three year plan. ERIC Document Reproduction Service, no. ED342535.

Mac Iver, D., and J. Epstein. (1991). Responsive practices in the middle grades: Teacher teams, advisory groups, remedial instruction, and school transition programs. *American Journal of Education* 99(4): 587–621.

Maeroff, G. (1993). Building teams to rebuild schools. *Phi Delta Kappan* 74(7): 512–519.

Oches, B. (1989). Teacher assistance teams: A process for democratic teachers. ERIC Document Reproduction Service, no. ED310541.

ADDITIONAL WEB RESOURCES

U.S. Department of Education. "School-Based Reform Lessons from a National Study: A Guide for School Reform Teams." www.ed.gov/pubs/Reform/index.html. "This guide was developed by members of the working group for the study of effective school programs and reforms for the U.S. Department of Education. "The guide is a resource for teachers and school administrators in the development and implementation of school-based reforms. Potential reform strategies and lessons learned from a national study of school-based reform are provided in this guide."

Fitzpatrick, A. "School Improvement through Teacher Decision Making." *Northwest Regional Educational Laboratory.* www.nwrel.org/scpd/sirs/8/s030.html. "In this article, Northwest Regional Educational Laboratory provides a strong case for effective leadership and decision making in the complex process of school improvement. The site outlines practices that have been shown to foster positive student achievement and effective outcomes."

"The Basics of Team Building." www.teamtechnology.co.uk/tt/h-articl/tb-basic.htm. "This article introduces some of the basic concepts of team building, asking such questions as, What is a team? and What is team building? It also explains some of the basic ideas behind improving the performance of teams."

"Team Building: Developing a Productive Team." www.ianr.unl.edu/pubs/Misc/cc352.htm. "This Web publication by the University of Nebraska Cooperative Extension Service provides a series of team-building concepts. It includes a list of characteristics of good team building as well as an evaluation instrument for team effectiveness."

Bangert, A., and G. Clayton. (2001). "Facilitating Teacher Assistance Teams: Key Questions." *NASSP Bulletin* 85(626). www.nassp.org/news/bltn_tchr_asst901.html. "Emphasis on problem development and analysis, and plan development and evaluation. 'Direct participation by the principal . . . in the Teaching Assistance Teams (TATs) is considered crucial.'"

National Association of Secondary School Principals (NASSP). (2000). "Portrait of the 'Ideal Principal': Context and Self." *NASSP Bulletin* 84(617) (September). www.nassp.org/news/bltn_portrait.htm. "NASSP provides an idealized view of the principal's role, which ignores both the importance that context plays and the unique and dynamic quality of individual principals."

CHAPTER 6

Persistence and Attitude

A persistent person can be defined as one who continues to follow the same course of action, no matter what. Persistent people never give up and keep trying with little regard to obstacles and problems along the path. Persistence is omnipotent; it is the force that creates success within people. An example of such persistence is reflected and evidenced in one of America's heroic figures, Abraham Lincoln. The evidence of his persistence is revealed in the following:

> Lincoln was defeated when he ran for the Illinois House of Representatives in 1832. But he was victorious in the House race in 1834, and was then reelected for three consecutive terms. He was defeated when he ran for the U.S. House of Representatives in 1843, then ran successfully for a House seat in 1846. Abe was defeated for the Senate in 1855 and Vice Presidency in 1856. Again, in 1858, Lincoln sought election to the Senate and was defeated. As a reward for his persistence, Lincoln was elected President of the United States in 1860. (Sullivan, 1987)

Administrators and teachers have a duty to assume the responsibility of developing a campus attitude of persistence and doing whatever it takes to make students successful. If educators do not obtain support from the home, then the teaching team is the only thing left to make a difference in the life of a child. In every school there needs to be an underlying attitude of "we will *persist longer than they resist*." The moment we stop being persistent, the negative behavior or lack of responsibility on the part of the student becomes positively reinforced. When a negative behavior is positively reinforced long enough, it then becomes the normal behavior of the individual. Breaking the cycle of students not doing homework and not studying for tests is very difficult, but *persistence* is the key. Educators must take on the following attitude: if we assign something to be done, then it is important that we see that it gets done. Only when this is etched in administrators', teachers', and students' daily routines have we accomplished the task of creating the "doing whatever it takes" attitude necessary to ensure academic success.

PERSISTENCE WITH ASSIGNED WORK

All members of the academic team will need to contribute to the persistence process. Practical interventions are essential to bring to an end the student practice of not doing assignments, not reading assigned works, and not studying for exams. Creating an array of interventions that work for your school will be the key to bringing the problem to a workable level. Mandatory before- and after-school student work and study sessions manned by teachers, study buddies, and/or trained parent volunteers can make a significant impact in a short period of time. Most high-school students are motivated by time, and cutting into that time with these mandatory before- and after-school tutorials can bring the acquired behavior of apathy toward schoolwork to a screeching halt very quickly. Several other promising practices and interventions will be discussed in the next chapter.

POSITIVE REINFORCEMENT OF STUDENTS AND TEACHERS

Once the first-stage interventions begin to make an impact, the practice of positively reinforcing small incremental student successes should be in place. Secondary teachers need training and modeling of positive reinforcement and motivational techniques. Quality staff-development activities in reinforcement as well as motivational theory connected to best practices are sound investments toward a thriving intervention. Ninth-grade students, like all other people, respond well to positive reinforcement for their efforts. Swift, sincere, and sustained positive reinforcement of students will breed more of the same behaviors.

Teachers, volunteers, and other individuals involved in the intervention program will also need to be reinforced for their hard work and persistence. Some sort of system of recognition and rewards should be a regular part of the improvement program. Regular feedback on the improvement in reducing failure rates is motivational, and teachers with significant gains will continue to improve if recognized and reinforced for their attention to the tasks at hand. Far too often the efforts of teaching professionals go unnoticed, which creates a lack of drive and effort to succeed. School climate and culture will improve greatly with regular sincere reinforcement from the campus leader and central office.

THE CHANGE PROCESS

The process of changing our schools to facilitate student success and changing the paradigm of education to prepare students for the future they face in this century rather than the preparation for employment that existed in the 1950s is a monumental task at best. Convincing teachers and staff that students must be prepared for their future rather than our past is sometimes an enormously overwhelming experience. Moreover, one of the best arguments for changing our schools is that the time for which our schools have been designed will no longer exist in just a few short years.

Change in the real world of employment happens rapidly. Teachers are no longer teaching Wally and Beaver with a stay-at-home mother and a father who works an eight-hour day. The students in the system today are different from those just ten years or five years ago. New strategies and methods are essential to keep pace with the ever-changing society. Children in the schools of today will encounter a world of more advanced technology, nanotechnology, and biotechnology employment. The next generation of students will most likely encounter six to ten career changes, not job changes—career changes requiring lifelong learning capabilities. Schools that remain in the solid-matter state, refusing to adapt to the changing world, will eventually be forced out of business.

Learning takes place when learners regard what one needs to know as relevant to their lives; when they feel that their teachers are committed to student success; and when the institutional environment allows for differences in learning methods and styles and is in harmony with the diverse needs and interests of the learner (Parnell, 1985). Connecting learning to the real world and providing relevant learning activities is only one answer to the problems we face in schools today. Educational innovation worthy of investigation is found in the works of Carl Glickman and others (2003) who have fostered the service learning network. When children, especially adolescents to early adults, connect learning to community and relevant activity, a whole new world of motivation for education opens in their minds.

Persistence and resilience are possible solutions to some of the problems facing our schools. Educators must prepare students for the future as lifelong learners, a future in which the average person may be forced into as many as twenty different jobs and will probably change careers as many as six to ten times, of which four or more have not been conceived by the world of work at this time.

DOING WHATEVER IT TAKES

Perhaps the greatest challenge facing a campus leader is the development of a unitary attitude among teachers and staff to do whatever it takes to facilitate student achievement and academic success. It takes time, persistence, and collaboration between and among all members of the organization to develop a positive climate conducive to progress. A great campus leader will become a walking and talking billboard for *doing whatever it takes*. Every piece of written communication (memos, e-mail, newsletters, etc.) should be inscribed with "doing whatever it takes." Constant reminders and reinforcement for the *whatever it takes* attitude is paramount to sustaining efforts (figure 6.1). Quality instructional leaders cultivate the culture of the school community and strive to build positive relationships among and between students, teachers, and staff members. Persistence is crucial in the effort to transition an entire staff attitude. Without a doubt, days will come when even the best teachers and administrators will want to give up the ship; however, reminding yourself to keep the "persist longer than they resist" attitude will sustain the quest for school improvement.

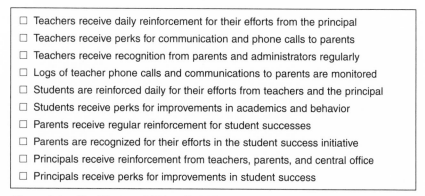

□ Teachers receive daily reinforcement for their efforts from the principal
□ Teachers receive perks for communication and phone calls to parents
□ Teachers receive recognition from parents and administrators regularly
□ Logs of teacher phone calls and communications to parents are monitored
□ Students are reinforced daily for their efforts from teachers and the principal
□ Students receive perks for improvements in academics and behavior
□ Parents receive regular reinforcement for student successes
□ Parents are recognized for their efforts in the student success initiative
□ Principals receive reinforcement from teachers, parents, and central office
□ Principals receive perks for improvements in student success

Figure 6.1.   *The Whatever It Takes Checklist*

The noble effort of doing whatever it takes can go a long way in building lasting constructive relationships and improvement toward greater student success and, ultimately, higher graduation rates.

ORGANIZATIONAL ATTITUDE ADJUSTMENT

Development of a new organizational climate requires a willingness to take risks among all professional educators, even when it is outside the boundaries of their basic personality strengths or counterproductive tendencies or both. Changing the basic ingrained climate of an organization is a journey with a long timeline. Sustained improvement in school and organizational climate sometimes take years of growth with pain. In theory and practice, about 25 percent of an organization will change or adapt to new innovations almost overnight and as many as 50 percent will venture into the waters of change very quickly after the initial group; however, approximately 25 percent of most organizations will in some way or form resist change. The 25 percent that are reluctant to change will require the greatest amounts of energy and commitment to implement new innovations. With a strong climate of commitment to improvement, meaningful staff development, and positive outcomes, an overwhelming majority of the laggards in the lower quartile will eventually get on the bandwagon or leave the organization to impede progress in places where they are allowed to feel more comfortable.

CONCLUSION

Administrators will be in a constant mode of diagnosis and assessment of the staff members' developmental stages to determine the correct leadership style applicable to the situation. The leader should provide constant feedback and support for educators in transition. To maintain positive attitudes, sincere positive reinforcement should be consistent and intermittently dispersed throughout the process of organization climate change. Once the transformation is made to "we do whatever it takes to ensure student success," continuous reinforcement will be necessary to sustain the change. Great school leaders will create the conditions for positive changes in education and sustain the process through constant diagnosis, continuous reinforcement, and untiring persistence.

REFERENCES

Glickman, C., et al. (2003). *The national service-learning partnership.* Available online at servicelearningcommission.org/leadership/nslpnewaddr.html [accessed January 16, 2003].

Parnell, D. (1985). *The neglected majority.* Washington, D.C.: Community College Press.

Sullivan, G. (1987). *Facts and fun about the presidents.* New York: Scholastic. Excerpt retrieved from Scholastic website. Available online at teacher.scholastic.com/researchtools/articlearchives/civics/presid/fun/ prhang.htm [accessed October 5, 2002].

ADDITIONAL WEB RESOURCES

"Savvy and Persistence." *Role of Leadership in Sustaining School Reform: Voices from the Field* (July 1996). www.ed.gov/pubs/Leadership/ch2d.html. "This article on the U.S. Department of Education's website links to several excellent resources on the topics of managing day-to-day school issues, managing long-term school issues, maintaining a good relationship with the central office, and maintaining a good relationship with the community."

"Teacher Behaviors That Encourage Persistence." www.dpi.state.wi.us/dpi/ dlsea/equity/pdf/persist.pdf. "A checklist of teacher behaviors for ensuring persistence in their students."

Massell, D., M. Kirst, and M. Hoppe. (1997). "Persistence and Change: Standards-Based Systemic Reform in Nine States." Consortium for Policy Research in Education (CPRE), RB-21. www.edsource.org/edu_sta_res_ massell2.cfm. "This policy brief highlights findings of a study conducted by CPRE researchers to examine the evolution of standards-based reform in nine states in 1994–1995. Researchers interviewed state and district policymakers and educators in California, Connecticut, Florida, Georgia, Kentucky, Minnesota, New Jersey, South Carolina, and Texas."

Meader, P. (2000). "The Effects of Continuing Goal-Setting on Persistence in a Math Classroom." *Focus on the Basics* 4(A). www.gse.harvard. edu/~nsall/fob/2000/meader.html. "A research team surveyed students who were successful in completing their objectives. They found that students felt that setting goals helped them in their persistence. The team conducted the project by observing what effect continuing goal setting in a math class would have on learner persistence."

CHAPTER 7

Interventions and Innovations

After ten years of qualitative research, data gathering, engagement in professional dialogue, and on-site campus visits with students, teachers, administrators, and counselors, I arrive at the conclusion that a significant number of ninth-grade failure rates can be attributed to administrative brain freezes and teacher attitudes. Too many administrators assign first-year or inexperienced teachers with limited skills to ninth-grade students. These students are facing the greatest challenges in their high-school careers and need teachers with experience and a repertoire of successful practices. In addition, teachers assigned to teach ninth grade should have training in a variety of strategies proven to work with transitioning students. Some studies have found that teachers with middle-school and/or elementary-level experiences work well with first-year high-school students.

Support specialists in the areas of counseling, curriculum, and instruction have proven to be beneficial in programs around the country. Teachers assigned to high-school transition students need a plethora of resources in an effort to provide quality instruction. Curriculum content specialists trained in transition issues are essential for success. Instructional support is another high-need resource. Instructional specialists with expertise in ninth grade should be a part of the team-building concept. Finally, students in the transition year need a high level of counseling and guidance assistance and connection with a caring adult with quality training in the obstacles, perils, and difficulties faced by ninth-grade children. High human resource costs are associated with these support personnel; ultimately, however, the cost-effectiveness is balanced with the gains made in the number of students who remain in school and successfully move to the tenth grade.

TEACHER ASSIGNMENT

One simple intervention with little or no costs attached is to stop the practice of assigning inexperienced, poorly trained, and unskilled teachers to the ninth grade. This group of students is in the greatest transitional period of their school career and need the expertise of highly skilled and experienced teachers with a "do whatever it takes" attitude toward education. A difficulty exists in creating the environment where experienced teachers are intrinsically motivated for taking on the challenge that ninth-grade students bring, but it is a key element in changing the pattern of failure. Experienced teachers sometimes develop the attitude that they have "paid their dues" and now deserve only the best or most motivated students, yet the rewards of teaching can be acquired and even deepened by teaching students with the greatest needs. Exemplary campus leaders will sell the idea that the best teachers accept the challenge of ninth-grade students and utilize their repertoire of skills to change the pattern of failure. When experienced teachers see the rewards connected to teaching ninth graders, campus leaders will have little difficulty in recruiting the best instructors for the most rewarding experience of their careers. Recognition and reinforcement are of utmost importance to develop the culture and campus attitude that the best teachers belong with the kids that need the most help. The intervention of placing the most caring, skilled, and talented teachers with ninth graders may be the single best and simplest intervention, and the central office will love it due to the no-cost factor.

TUTORIALS WITHIN THE SCHOOL DAY

A common intervention suggested by teachers and administrators to parents of children who struggle in school is tutoring. The limitation connected to this intervention is that many parents do not possess the financial resources to hire tutors and lack the academic skills necessary to do a good job of tutoring their own child. Creating a time in the school day for peer and teacher tutoring is a practical solution to the problem. Creative administrators can always find a few minutes here and there to have a pep rally or an assembly. It should be just as easy to find time for an organized, supervised, and successful tutorial period a few days a week. Student-rewards systems and breaks could be a viable reward for peer tutoring and completion of assignments on time. The key to this intervention is organization, persistence, and creativity. Constant monitoring of progress and the ability to admit that a component of the intervention is not working as well as expected and then making necessary changes to sustain the process are proactive measures to consider. Again, persistence is a supreme factor in continuous progress toward reducing the failure problem among ninth-grade students.

TUTORIALS OUTSIDE THE SCHOOL DAY

Not only are before- and after-school mandatory tutorials beneficial in putting the brakes on failure; they can also contribute to sustaining the trend of failure reduction. Communicating this requirement to parents long before implementation is essential to gaining support and preparing them for the inconvenience it may impose on their lives. Stressing the long-term benefits to the education of their child will go a long way toward gaining support. A campaign to enlist parent and student volunteers to properly staff the before- and after-school program also carries an element of importance. Grant funding is sometimes available to initiate an extended-day program for at-risk or other special populations of students.

In defense of secondary teachers, university preparation programs continue to deliver a heavy dose of subject matter at the expense of sound instructional pedagogy, best practice, and effective teaching methods. Ninth-grade teachers need a significant amount of skill in methods that work with transitional students. Rookie and other inexperienced teachers, for the most part, lack the necessary skills to successfully deal with the challenges thrown at them by even the best of freshmen students. A special group of skilled educational professionals with exceptional attitudes are required to make gains in the area of ninth-grade failure and retention in grade level.

First-year high-school students should have skills in responsible be-haviors, but the cold reality is that they are void of responsible behavior in most instances. Far too many educators have the attitude that these young people should be totally responsible and then suffer the conse-quences for students' ineptitude or lack of attention to their studies. This attitude is in conflict with the needs of the students in transition from a loosely structured exploratory middle/junior high school to a highly structured educational unit with a lack of support services needed by 14- and 15-year-olds in the midst of puberty, not to mention identity crises.

Schools throughout the country face the same problem in regard to high rates of ninth-grade failure. Many of these schools have imple-mented promising interventions based on successful best practices or sound research.

EXTENDED-DAY LEARNING

The expectation that all children will or can learn is a great statement. Yet a key element missing here is that they can or will learn all at the same time and at the same pace. Having taught technology to graduate students, teachers, and administrators for some time now, I have be-come keenly aware that everyone does not learn at the same rate or in the same time frame. For many adults and students in our classrooms, some concepts just take a little longer to grasp. A strong case can be made for extended-day learning if we all acknowledge the reality that some students learn faster or slower than their regular education aver-age peers. Schools need to adapt to this newfound realization by pro-viding for the differences in learning capability with more instructional and practice time either during the school day, after school hours, in the evening twilight, or on weekends. Many successful ninth-grade schools are adopting this innovation to enhance student success, improve ac-countability scores, and increase graduation rates.

EXTENDED-YEAR LEARNING

Extended-year services have become mandatory for some special edu-cation children with special learning needs. Extended-year learning and services are proven to be a great idea for regular education nonhandi-capped students as well. With the accountability and high-stakes test-ing ball rolling across the country, the need for innovations in and fund-ing for extended-year learning services will become a high priority. In Texas, graduation rate is a component of the public-school accounta-bility system. In an effort to increase the number of students moving from grade nine to grade ten, more and more schools are implementing extended-year programs to address achievement deficiencies as well as the accumulation of course credits to move to the next grade level. Many designs and configurations of extended-year programs exist with the primary goal of raising the accountability rating; however, the true underlying benefit is more students graduating from high schools with higher levels of competency in the key academic areas ready to enter higher education, the military, or the workforce.

MASTERY LEARNING

Basically, Benjamin Bloom's message to the educational world is to fo-cus on target attainment and to abandon a horse-race model of school-ing that has as its major aim the identification of those who are swiftest. Speed is not the issue—achievement or mastery is—and it is that model that should be employed in trying to develop educational programs for the young (Eisner, 2000).

Bloom recognized that what was important in education was not that students should be compared, but that they should be helped to achieve the goals of the curriculum they were studying. The teaching process needed to be geared toward designing tasks that would progressively and ineluctably lead to the realization of the objectives that defined the over-all goals of the curriculum. The variable that needed to be addressed, as Bloom saw it, was time. It made no pedagogical sense to expect all stu-dents to take the same amount of time to achieve the same objectives. There were individual differences among students, and the important thing was to accommodate those differences to promote learning rather than to hold time constant and expect some students to fail. Education was not a race. In addition, students were allowed—indeed encour-aged—to help one other. Feedback and correction were immediate. In short, Bloom was applying in a very rational way the basic assumptions embraced by those who believe the educational process should be geared toward the realization of educational objectives. He believed that such an approach to curriculum, to teaching, and to assessment would enable virtually all youngsters to achieve success in school (Eisner, 2000).

The mastery learning model is exceptionally effective when properly implemented. In studies where strategies have been refined, 90 percent of the mastery learning students have achieved as well as the top 20 percent of the nonmastery learning students (Wegener, n.d.). Mastery learning is achieved through the establishment of a criterion level of performance held to represent "mastery" of a given skill or concept, frequent assessment of student progress toward the mastery criterion, and provision of corrective instruction to enable students who do not initially meet the mastery criterion to do so on later parallel assessment. Mastery learning approaches are geared toward the organization of time and resources to ensure that most students are able to master instructional objectives (Mendiola and Soto, 2001).

Restructuring the learning environments by implementing Benjamin Bloom's mastery learning process is only one essential element in the process of improving student success. Mastery learning is a change of attitude as well as a strategy that requires a considerable amount of staff training. Adoption of the philosophy that we reteach and retest students until they master a concept is key to the success of this process. Effectiveness and quality of staff development critically influence effects on student retention and achievement. The research available on the mastery learning process is relevant, reliable, and valid.

Southern Regional Education Board (SREB) implemented the High Schools That Work network and has developed a set of meaningful solutions for students in the transition year with different learning capacities. According to SREB (n.d.), the following are key components of the successful and innovative program:

- *High expectations:* Setting higher expectations and getting more students to meet them.
- *Vocational studies:* Increasing access to intellectually challenging vocational and technical studies, with a major emphasis on using high-level mathematics, science, language arts, and problem-solving

skills in the modern workplace and in preparation for continued learning.

- *Academic studies:* Increasing access to academic studies that teach the essential concepts from the college preparatory curriculum by encouraging students to use academic content and skills to address real-world projects and problems.
- *Program of study:* Having students complete a challenging program of study with an upgraded academic core and a major.
- *Work-based learning:* Giving students and their parents the choice of a system that integrates school- and work-based learning. The system should span high-school and postsecondary studies and should be planned by educators, employers, and employees.
- *Teachers working together:* Having an organization, structure, and schedule giving academic and vocational teachers the time to plan and deliver integrated instruction aimed at teaching high-level academic and technical content.
- *Students actively engaged:* Getting every student involved in rigorous and challenging learning.
- *Guidance:* Involving each student and his or her parents in a guidance and advising system that ensures the completion of an accelerated program of study with an in-depth academic or vocational-technical major.
- *Extra help:* Providing a structured system of extra help to enable students who may lack adequate preparation to complete an accelerated program of study that includes high-level academic and technical content.
- *Keeping score:* Using student assessment and program evaluation data to improve continuously the school climate, organization, management, curricula, and instruction to advance student learning and to recognize students who meet both curriculum and performance goals. (SREB, n.d.)

CONCLUSION

Designing ultimately successful interventions with adequate innovation is a journey that may consume years of persistent monitoring, evaluation, and adjustment (figure 7.1). School leaders should always be mindful that it is a journey, not just a series of tasks. Quality leaders will persist through the pain and agony of transition while continually praising the efforts of the people in the trenches. Developing interventions such as extended-day learning, extended-year learning, mastery learning, and/or peer tutoring will contribute to the success effort. However, the commonsense practice of recruiting and assigning teachers who are experienced, successful, and caring does more than contribute to success—it perpetuates success. Searching for and implementing the key components that swing the pendulum of failure in the opposite direction will take time, although the end result will be realized in the living messages—the students—sent into the world with a quality education to take on careers of the information age, the biotechnical age, and beyond.

☐ Establish teaming with teachers and students

☐ Establish peer- and teacher-assisted tutorials

☐ Design and implement a comprehensive extended-day and extended-year program

☐ Synchronize teaching, homework, and testing

☐ Train teachers in mastery learning strategies

☐ Implement mastery learning in every subject area

☐ Train teachers well in cooperative and collaborative team learning

☐ Establish relevant, cooperative thematic units throughout the year

☐ Establish new grading policies and procedures for ninth-grade students

☐ Train teachers in alternative assessment practices such as portfolios

☐ Implement interdisciplinary or thematic teaching

☐ Design and implement an exemplary counseling and guidance program

☐ Vertically align and connect the ninth-grade and middle-school curriculum

☐ Align, focus, and connect the curriculum across the ninth-grade level

☐ Allow for more elective credits at the ninth-grade level

    ◦ Shift the heavier academic load to the tenth, eleventh, and twelfth grades

    ◦ Invert the curriculum as much as possible

☐ Assign teachers to the ninth grade that have expertise and a passion for student success

☐ Sincerely praise teachers and students for their continuous improvement or efforts

☐ Make teaching, learning, and school fun again!

Figure 7.1.   *Successful Innovations and Interventions Checklist*

REFERENCES

Eisner, E. (2000). Benjamin Bloom 1913–99. *Prospects: Quarterly Review of Comparative Education* (Paris, UNESCO: International Bureau of Education), 30(3). Available online at www.ibe.unesco.org/International/Publications/Thinkers/ThinkersPdf/bloome.pdf [accessed September 4, 2002].

Mendiola, C., and A. Soto. (2001). [Techchallenge] Benjamin Bloom. Available online at listserv.utep.edu/pipermail/techchallenge/2001-January/000615.html [accessed September 4, 2002].

Southern Regional Education Board. (n.d.). High schools that work: Key practices. Available online at www.sreb.org/programs/hstw/background/keypractices.asp [accessed September 5, 2002].

Wegener, D. P. (n.d.). An opportunity for reform. Available online at www.delweg.com/library/cbtwing/cbtmain.htm [accessed September 4, 2002].

ADDITIONAL WEB RESOURCES

"Benjamin Bloom's Taxonomy of Thinking." www.cobb.k12.ga.us/~mtbethel/Classes/target/Bloom.htm. "This page from the Mt. Bethel Elementary School (Marietta, Ga.) website explains the components of Benjamin Bloom's Taxonomy of Thinking: knowledge, comprehension, application, analysis, synthesis, and evaluation."

Wegener, D. P. "An Opportunity for Reform." www.delweg.com/dpwessay/reform.htm. "This essay connects Benjamin Bloom's mastery learning concept to distance education."

"Mastery Learning." *Free World Research.* www.wccta.net/gallery/fwr/maslea.htm. "A great place to retrieve a concise definition of terms generated by Bloom and others on the concept of mastery learning and higher order thinking related to Bloom's taxonomy."

Hope Hall School, Rochester, N.Y. hopehall.org/mil.shtml. "The site outlines the components of the Mastery in Learning© Program and explains the specialized approach to learning and teaching for students with special learning needs."

Gardner, H. "Multiple Intelligences." tip.psychology.org/gardner.html. "The theory of multiple intelligences suggests that there are a number of distinct forms of intelligence that each individual possesses in varying degrees. Gardner proposes seven primary forms: linguistic, musical, logical-mathematical, spatial, body-kinesthetic, intrapersonal (e.g., insight, metacognition), and interpersonal (e.g., social skills)."

"Module 1: What Is Mastery Learning?" *Front End Analysis: Mastery Learning.* syllabus.syr.edu/IDE/maeltigi/ide713/toolbox/class97/bragg/tutorial/modulea/indexa.html. "Who transformed Mastery Learning into a powerful instructional theory that offers a new approach to student learning? Benjamin S. Bloom, John B. Carroll."

Bourduas, F. Sheridan College Professional Development Recipient report. www.sheridanc.on.ca/acadserv/pd/edpsycourse.html. "Basic skills through mastery learning. An interview with Benjamin S. Bloom."

Southern Regional Education Board (SREB). *High Schools That Work.* www.sreb.org/programs/hstw/hstwindex.asp. "A superb site that details the components and research related to SREB's High Schools That Work program. It is the largest and oldest of the SREB's seven school-improvement initiatives for high-school and middle-grade leaders and teachers."

CHAPTER 8

Professional Staff Development

Of all the things educational leaders accomplish in the name of organizational improvement, none can have a greater influence than well-planned and sustained professional staff development. Teachers need quality long-term development in effective teaching strategies such as interdisciplinary instruction, learning styles, teaming, technology integration, and cooperative learning strategies. Continuous high-quality staff development rather than a one-time "shot in the arm" type of training is necessary to sustain improvement and effective implementation of innovative teaching methods such as learning styles and use of technological innovations.

This is a wonderful opportunity to utilize teaching staff with the best teaching strategies at this level. Professional staff development generated at the campus level that is directly related to the problem on that particular campus is a key element in improvement. When teachers are actively and physically involved in either conducting or selecting staff development related to the specific problems in their classrooms, the probability of buy-in and implementation are significantly increased. Research, as well as Senate Bill No. 1, support site-based involvement in staff development, yet we continue to provide staff development that is selected by high-level administration or central office personnel.

Training may be the foremost incremental factor that affects the success or failure of an academic-teaming intervention program. Teams must receive the proper training, and it should be directed at the team-building concept to provide practical experiences that will enhance the ability of the team to intervene in key situations to facilitate success with students. Furthermore, the training process should be systematic with regular follow-ups and adjustments to the program as needed. Finally, team effectiveness should be evaluated on a regular basis and should focus on the impact that the teams are having on student and teacher progress toward high achievement as well as social success within the school setting.

Teachers and support staff are a critical link connecting the curriculum and students; consequently, professional development is an indispensable component in the developmental process of collegial teacher leadership. Professional development activities foster leadership development within teachers. Moreover, meaningful and connected development activities further the probability of implementation and improvement of the instructional program. Teaching professionals become motivated by the desire to increase connected student learning. School administrators need to initiate an environment conducive to teacher growth with improvement in curriculum and instruction delivery. Teachers should have the opportunity to rethink their notion about the nature of science, be willing to develop new views about how students learn, construct new classroom learning environments, and create new expectations about student outcomes (Nelson and Hammerman, 1996).

Principals and teachers are saddled with the challenge of design and implementation of professional development programs that influence or have an impact on effective teaching practices. The wealth of information, research, and knowledge of professional development strategies continues to expand exponentially. Research and literature suggest precise methodologies that should positively influence professional development programs. Research by Rhoton et al. (1999) identifies selected techniques for improvement of professional development. The first step is to address issues of concern recognized by teachers themselves. One-size-fits-all professional development does not, in fact, meet the needs of all teachers. Teachers at different stages in their teaching careers will require professional development to meet their specific needs. Effective staff development is connected to classroom practices. It should address issues and immediate concerns relevant to the classroom, such as teaching practices and working with groups that differ in ability and motivation. The process should include sustained support and take place over an extended period of time.

Lasting change usually occurs only when teachers are given the sufficient time, resources, and training to carry out the innovation. A quality plan will help teachers learn content in new ways. These experiences allow teachers to genuinely address change and renewal and reach beyond the "make and take" workshop and the "idea swap" session to more global, theoretical conversations that focus on teachers' understanding of the processes of science teaching and learning and of the students they teach. Professional development should challenge pedagogical beliefs and practices. Teacher perceptions about student learning, confidence in subject matter understanding, and pedagogical beliefs will affect student learning. Research supports the premise that professional development promotes incremental change. Although large-scale change may be needed, incremental change allows teachers to retain existing effective practices. As a final point, quality professional development encourages collaboration among teaching professionals and fosters the team concept.

GUIDELINES FOR PROFESSIONAL DEVELOPMENT SUCCESS

As a result of the research of Guskey (1995), guidelines for developing professional development were coined. Guskey contends that due to the powerful and dynamic influence of context, it is impossible to make precise statements about the elements of effective professional development. The best that can be offered are procedural guidelines deemed critical to the professional development process. The guidelines reflect a framework for developing that optimal mix of professional development processes and technologies. Evidence indicates that neglecting the issues described in these guidelines at best will limit success and, at worst, will result in programs and activities that fail to bring about significant or enduring change.

Guideline one asserts the need to recognize change as both an individual and an organizational process. An important lesson learned from the past is that we cannot improve schools without improving the skills and abilities of the professional educators within them. In other words, we must see change as an individual process and be willing to invest in the intellectual capital of those individuals who staff our schools (Wise, 1991).

Guideline two expresses the need to think big, but start small. Successful professional development programs are those that approach change in a gradual and incremental fashion. The effort must not be so ambitious that the programs require too much too soon; they do need to be sufficient enough to challenge professionals and pique interest (McLaughlin, 1990).

Guideline three advocates that educators work in teams to maintain support. The discomfort that accompanies change is greatly compounded if the individuals involved perceive that they have no say in the process or if they feel isolated and detached in their implementation efforts. For this reason, it is imperative that all aspects of professional development be fashioned to involve teams of individuals working together.

Guideline four articulates the inclusion of procedures for feedback on results. Personal feedback on results can be provided in a variety of ways, depending on the context. Formative assessments also offer teachers specific feedback on the effectiveness of their application of newly acquired knowledge. The methods used to obtain feedback, for example, must not be disruptive of instructional procedures. Timing issues are also critical, for it is unfair to expect too much too soon from those involved in implementation.

The basic premise of guideline five is to provide follow-up, support, and pressure. Support coupled with pressure is vital for continuation and sustained improvements. Support allows those engaged in the difficult process of implementation to tolerate the anxiety of occasional failures. Pressure for change is essential to move people who may be particularly resistant to change.

Finally, guideline six advocates the integration of programs. Doyle (1992), Sarason (1990), and others emphasize that coordinating programs and combining ideas release great energy in the improvement process. Fullan (1992) stresses that "schools are not in the business of managing single innovations; they are in the business of contending with multiple innovations simultaneously" (p. 19).

Conclusively, these procedural guidelines are not new and are not considered revolutionary. They probably appear obvious to those with extensive experience in professional development. As evident as they may be, it is unusual to find professional development efforts today that are designed and implemented with thorough attention to these guidelines. Indeed, it is atypical to find professional development endeavors that evaluate the implementation of these guidelines in terms of effects on student learning.

INNOVATIONS IN PROFESSIONAL DEVELOPMENT

Professional development is being transformed with the invention of advanced technologies and Internet capabilities. We are witnessing a new era of innovative and interactive "learn anywhere anytime" professional development resources, which are being developed with the busy teacher in mind. Online staff development is becoming commonplace in the real world of education. The Association for Supervision and Curriculum Development website (www.ascd.org) has a comprehensive set of online learning modules geared toward busy educators and schools with limited staff development resources. Educational innovators are entering the marketplace daily in an effort to provide professional educational development services for profit in a real-time environment. As the technologies continue to develop, it is only to be expected that professional development in new and innovative formats will emerge. Some of the innovations utilized in the present and projected to expand in the future are as follows:

- *Teleconferencing:* Two-way, audio or video to remote sites.
- *Television and interactive television:* Provides teachers with specific courses of study.
- *Distance learning courses:* Provides Internet-based instruction on selected topics.
- *Electronic mail:* Listservs or direct connectivity with other teaching professionals.
- *Videotapes or videodiscs:* Allow teachers to investigate new teaching practices
- *CD-ROMs:* May include materials, video, audio, and useful educational resources.
- *Tools for group work:* GroupSystems, from Ventana Corporation, provides a computer-based support tool for facilitation of same-time, same-place, as well as same-time, different-place meetings.

Participants are linked together through computers and the main GroupSystems program that is monitored by a facilitator. During a session, participants can switch from discussions to online group or individual work. (Loucks-Horsley, 1998)

UTILIZING STUDY GROUPS

An effective strategy for development and growth of professional staff is currently evolving and expanding exponentially. It is a bold concept to think that teachers might learn from each other and implement improvement strategies based on their own innovative ideas or expertise discussed in a study-group meeting. According to Rhoton et al. (1999), teachers consistently rank professional development activities that take place close to the working environment as the most important, whereas workshops by outside experts are ranked as the least important. Change usually occurs in small pockets within the school. The primary premise of the concept of study groups is that members are organized around a specific topic of importance to the participating teachers. Same-grade teachers may develop a study group to acquire knowledge and skills related to implementation of curricular or instructional topics, concepts, or strategies. In a span of time the study group convenes to conduct, interpret, and discuss research. They may evaluate and present a variety of approaches to a specific problem or involve personnel resources with a high level of expertise in a given problematic area influencing student success. Makibbin and Sprague (1991) suggest four models for structuring study groups:

1. The implementation model is designed to support teachers' use of techniques recently learned in workshops or other short-term sessions.
2. The institutionalization model is used once teachers have already implemented new practices in the classroom and want to continue refining these practices.
3. Research-sharing groups are organized around discussions of recent research and how it relates to classroom practice.
4. Investigation study groups are a way for teachers to identify a topic they would like to research.

Success of study groups requires direct support from school administrators, not only for the time for the group to meet, but also for support for the endeavor itself. Administrators send a clear message about the importance of professional development for teachers if time is set aside during the school day for study groups to convene. Administrators can also offer support by providing access to additional resources, such as new technology or outside experts.

COLLEGIAL COACHING AND MENTORING

Collegial or peer coaching and mentoring are approaches that provide probable situations for collegial learning among teaching professionals. Coaching is an interactive opportunity for professional peer growth and development to evolve between teachers who possess knowledge, skill, and expertise in a variety of curricular or instructional areas. Mentoring is usually more directed and involves the sharing of expertise between a seasoned teaching professional and a less skillful colleague.

In times past, coaching targeted classroom observations and formative feedback from the peer coach. The concept of coaching has been expanded to include other activities, such as planning instruction, developing materials, and discussing the impact of teacher behavior on students (Showers and Joyce, 1996).

Mentors generally take on the roles of teacher, coach, role model, sponsor, guardian, and creator of opportunities. The literature on mentoring beginning teachers is substantial; research indicates that effective mentoring programs can lower the attrition rate for new teachers, significantly decreasing the length and trauma of their induction period into the profession (Newton et al., 1994).

RECOMMENDED NINTH-GRADE
PROFESSIONAL DEVELOPMENT

In reviewing programs for ninth-grade success and visiting with professional educators in and out of the classroom, it is concluded that some common problems exist in professional development activities. A select few of the recommended areas of need identified through discussions with people in the trenches are that teachers need professional growth in the following:

- Learning differences of students in a transition year
- Integration of technology to motivate the digital student
- Dealing with the problems associated with ninth-grade students
- Ninth-grade-specific instructional interventions
- Working with teams of teachers and students
- Learning disabilities and differences among students
- Heterogeneous group instructional techniques and innovations
- Successful discipline strategies and interventions
- Stress management while balancing teaching and life
- Time management and planning to maximize teaching

CONCLUSION

School leaders will need to implement innovative approaches to professional development that influence school climate as well as culture.

Ask the following questions:

☐ Can the staff development be directly related to the campus improvement plan?

☐ Is the staff development meaningful and relevant to those attending?

☐ Was the staff development generated by the teachers or teams of teachers?

☐ Will the staff development be funded properly to allow for continuation?

☐ Is there sufficient time allotted to maximize learning with and among the staff?

☐ Does the staff development foster collaboration and teaming?

☐ Does the staff development allow for practice and experience of the innovation?

☐ Does the staff development provide for follow-up observations by the trainer?

☐ Is the staff development activity based on best practices applicable to the school?

☐ Can the staff development be done by experts within your own school system?

☐ If not, have the best experts available been secured for the activity?

☐ Will the staff development lend itself to follow-up for sustained improvement?

☐ Will almost all teachers and staff view the staff development as a meaningful and worthwhile experience?

☐ Will evaluation data be distributed to all stakeholders to facilitate improvements for future staff development?

Figure 8.1.   *Professional Staff Development Questions Checklist*

Well-planned, organized, and orchestrated staff development plans need to be conducive to allowing implementation of best practices that allow teachers to interact within their professional peer group as well as outside of their own school domain (figure 8.1). The primary premise of the professional development plan will be to enhance student learning and to meet learner-centered connected goals. The transition school administrator should take a vow of commitment toward professional development that both nurtures and cultivates an innovative and enthusiastic learning environment among all team members.

REFERENCES

Doyle, D. P. (1992). The challenge, the opportunity. *Phi Delta Kappan* 73(7): 512–520.

Fullan, M. G. (1992). Visions that blind. *Educational Leadership* 49(5): 19–20.

Guskey, T. (1995). Results-oriented professional development: In search of an optimal mix of effective practices. Retrieved from North Central Regional Educational Laboratory website. Available online at www.ncrel.org/sdrs/areas/rpl_esys/pdlitrev.htm#Guidelines [accessed September 5, 2002].

Loucks-Horsley, S. (1998). Ideas that work: Mathematics professional development. Columbus, Ohio: Eisenhower National Clearinghouse. Retrieved from Eisenhower National Clearinghouse website. Available online at www.enc.org/professional/learn/ideas/math/document.shtm?input=ACQ-133273-3273_31 [accessed September 3, 2002].

Makibbin, S., and M. Sprague. (1991). Study groups: Conduit for reform. Paper presented at the annual meeting of the National Staff Development Council, St. Louis, Mo.

McLaughlin, M. W. (1990). The Rand change agent study revisited: Macro perspectives and micro realities. *Educational Researcher* 19(9): 1116.

Nelson, B. S., and J. M. Hammerman. (1996). Reconceptualizing teaching: The teaching and research program of the center for the development of teaching. In *Professional development in the reform era,* edited by M. W. McLaughlin and I. Oberman. New York: Teachers College Press.

Newton, A., K. Bergstrom, N. Brennan, K. Dunne, C. Gilbert, N. Ibarguen, M. Perez-Selles, and E. Thomas. (1994). *Mentoring: A resource and training guide for educators.* Andover, Mass.: The Regional Laboratory for Educational Improvement of the Northeast and Islands.

Rhoton, J., G. Madrazo, L. Motz, and E. Walton. (1999). Professional development: A major component in science teaching and learning. *Science Educator* 8(1): 1–8.

Sarason, S. (1990). *The predictable failure of educational reform.* San Francisco: Jossey-Bass.

Showers, B., and B. Joyce. (1996). The evolution of peer coaching. *Educational Leadership* 53(6): 12–16.

Wise, A. E. (1991). On teacher accountability. In *Voices from the field: Thirty expert opinions on "America 2000," the Bush administration strategy to "reinvent" America's schools* (pp. 23–24). Washington, D.C.: William T. Grant Foundation Commission on Work, Family and Citizenship and Institute for Educational Leadership.

ADDITIONAL WEB RESOURCES

North Central Regional Education Laboratory. "Professional Development: Staff Learning for Student Results." www.ncrel.org/pd/index.html. "Here you will find a full range of information geared to help you make professional development a bedrock of excellence in your school or district."

North Central Regional Education Laboratory. "Professional Development: Learning from the Best." www.ncrel.org/pd/toolkit.htm. "This is a toolkit for schools and districts based on the National Awards Program for Model Professional Development."

TERC. www.terc.edu/. Founded in 1965, TERC is a not-for-profit education research and development organization in Cambridge, Mass. "TERC's mission is to improve mathematics, science, and technology teaching and learning."

"Teacher Professionalism." *Apple.com.* www.apple.com/education/professionaldevelopment/. "Apple Computer supports the needs of teachers through Apple Learning Professional Development (ALPD) courses, as well as online courses, which help teachers get the most power from new technologies."

Duke, D. L., J. Bourdeaux, B. Epps, and T. Wilcox. "Ninth-Grade Transition Programs in Virginia: A Policy Perspective Paper from the Thomas Jefferson Center for Educational Design," University of Virginia. www.tjced.org/PDF%20files/9thgrade.pdf. "This Acrobat Reader file contains a study from a research team from the University of Virginia's Thomas Jefferson Center for Educational Design conducted with fourteen Virginia transition programs for ninth graders."

Center for Research on the Education of Students Placed at Risk (CRESPAR). "The Talent Development High School." depts.washington.edu/centerme/talent.htm#abstract. This web page provides highlights of the Talent Development High School model utilized at Patterson High School in Baltimore. The conceptual framework was initiated by Johns Hopkins educational research staff and professional educators from Patterson High. It focuses on the design and restructuring of high schools into smaller learning communities with attention on specific occupational pathways beginning with and targeting ninth-grade success.

Southern Regional Education Board (SREB). *High Schools That Work (HSTW)*. www.sreb.org/programs/hstw/hstwindex.asp. "High Schools That Work is the largest and oldest of the SREB's seven school-improvement initiatives for high-school and middle-grade leaders and teachers. More than 1,100 *HSTW* sites in twenty-seven states are using the *HSTW* framework of goals and key practices to raise student achievement."

AEL. "Professional Development That Improves Learning: A Winning Combination." www.ael.org/rel/quilt/overview.htm. "In the Questioning and Understanding to Improve Learning and Thinking (QUILT) model, effective questioning strategies create an environment that fosters higher order thinking, which results in greater mastery of concepts."

The Ontario Curriculum, Grades 9–12: Program Planning and Assessment, 2000. www.edu.gov.on.ca/eng/document/curricul/secondary/progplan/progplan.html. "This site was created by the Canadian Ministry of Education. The website contains policies on program planning, assessment, and evaluation for grades 9–12."

CHAPTER 9

Putting It All Together

Educators should examine the specific needs of students in an effort to develop a systematic plan to improve graduation rates and eliminate ninth-grade retention. A logical start to the improvement process would be to research, evaluate, and implement best practices and effective components of successful programs. Selecting highly qualified staff and engaging them in the development process of a comprehensive transition plan for students entering high school is essential to increase the probability of success.

DISTRICT COMMITMENT

District-level administrative leadership and local school board commitment in the form of financial support to ninth-grade transition is critical in the implementation and continuation of a quality program. Engagement in selling all facets of a new program should be the focus of all stakeholders. The support of parents, campus principals, and teachers is needed to facilitate realization of a concerted effort that eliminates ninth-grade failure and high dropout rates. School boards and superintendents hold the resource allocation power to implement or inhibit plans for improvement in graduation rates. These people will need to express real commitment to the facilities, personnel, and teaching resources that are required for gains in student achievement and success. Personnel cost is the greatest percentage expenditure for schools; therefore, the allocation of personnel resources and benefits is paramount to all other financial planning. Educational support personnel in the form of content specialists, instructional specialists, technology facilitators, counselors, and administrators are key elements in the start-up stage of a successful ninth-grade academy. Without this commitment, the transition endeavor will experience limited success at best or ultimately fail due to lack of resources and dedication to the program.

DEVELOPING THE PROGRAM

Incorporating the research-based best practices should be the basis at the developmental stage in creation of a transition plan for ninth grade. Once implemented, modifications can be made to adjust to individual needs of the student success initiative. Arrays of transition models and plans have been successfully implemented around the country. A number of ninth-grade transition schools follow the Johns Hopkins University Talent Development High School model. This model targets the development of small learning communities with an occupational pathway concentration in grades 10–12 and focuses on the ninth-grade academy concept. A team of educational research staff from Johns Hopkins University and professional educators at Patterson High School in Baltimore initiated the development and organization for the model. Exemplary achievement, high expectations, and academic rigor are at the base of this innovation in design and restructuring of high schools. According to the School District of Greenville County (2002), the following components should be a part of any good transition plan:

1. Efforts to ease the transition from middle to high school should start long in advance of the beginning of the ninth-grade year. Examples of some activities might include:
   - Small-group sessions with counselors
   - High-school teacher sessions with eighth graders
   - Teacher shadowing (eighth grade to ninth and ninth grade to eighth)
   - Summer camp for rising ninth graders
   - In-depth scheduling process

2. Improvement of one- and two-way communication between and among all interested parties should be a fundamental component. A few sample strategies include:

- Eighth-grade parent night at high school
- Parent meetings throughout ninth grade
- Team meetings with students and/or parents
- Report card suppers
- Regularly scheduled phone calls

3. Every school's plans should include ongoing, personal contact with every student throughout the ninth-grade year. Sample strategies to encourage this include:

- Advisory/homeroom classes with ongoing contact
- Meetings/conferences with individual students
- Use of agendas/weekly planners with follow-up
- Team/class spirit and identity efforts

4. Every school's plans should include advisory/homeroom classes with ongoing contact:

- Meetings/conferences with individual students
- Use of agendas/weekly planners with follow-up
- Team/class spirit and identity effort
- Isolated lunch for ninth graders
- Special clubs

5. Students identified as at risk of failure must be specifically targeted with prescriptive, proactive measures. Sample strategies include:

- Individual meetings with teachers/teacher team
- Special "catch-up" classes
- Teacher/peer tutors
- Use of agendas/weekly planners with follow-up
- Improvement awards (quarterly or ongoing, such as R.A.P. Club)
- Summer institutes (before and after ninth grade) to strengthen and teach skills

6. Teachers must use instructional strategies that keep students motivated and focused on learning; high expectations should be the norm for all students. Sample practices to encourage this include:

- Common planning times
- Interdisciplinary connections
- Consistent procedures, rules, and expectations

- Regular meetings to discuss and share instructional strategies
- Common files kept on students
- Development of a portfolio system

7. Evaluation of the success of strategies used should be based on measurable changes in areas of weakness. Data for evaluation of program strategies should include changes in the following:

- Grade-point averages of ninth graders
- Course failures of ninth graders
- Ninth-grade disciplinary referrals
- Percentage of students considered tenth graders at the end of the ninth grade
- Attitudes and expectations of students and parents

8. At the district level, several areas should be examined to provide consistency and reinforce high expectations for school:

- Specific guidelines and consistency are needed to determine accountability.
- Consistency is needed in procedural matters such as grading policies.
- The regular summer school program should be reviewed and revamped.

Incorporating elements of the aforementioned areas should facilitate relief of students' transition anxieties and foster success. Furthermore, it is recommended that every school allocate personnel resources to take responsibility for synchronizing efforts and serve as liaison for facilitating vertical and horizontal dialog among stakeholders.

HIGH SCHOOLS THAT WORK

Another successful reform initiative worthy of consideration was conceived by the Southern Regional Education Board (SREB) in 1987. It is coined the High Schools That Work initiative and has expanded to over half the states and over 1,100 campuses in America. The reform initiative combines challenging academic courses and modern career/technical studies to raise the achievement of career-bound high-school students. High Schools That Work is built on the belief that students following general and career/technical programs of study can master complex academic and technical concepts if schools create an environment that encourages students to make the effort to succeed (Bottoms, 2000). The key components of SREB's High Schools That Work model are as follows:

- *High expectations:* Setting higher expectations and getting more students to meet them.
- *Vocational studies:* Increasing access to intellectually challenging vocational and technical studies, with a major emphasis on using high-level mathematics, science, language arts, and problem-solving skills in the modern workplace and in preparation for continued learning.
- *Academic studies:* Increasing access to academic studies that teach the essential concepts from the college preparatory curriculum by encouraging students to use academic content and skills to address real-world projects and problems.
- *Program of study:* Having students complete a challenging program of study with an upgraded academic core and a major.
- *Work-based learning:* Giving students and their parents the choice of a system that integrates school- and work-based learning. The system should span high-school and postsecondary studies and should be planned by educators, employers, and employees.
- *Teachers working together:* Having an organization, structure, and schedule giving academic and vocational teachers the time to plan and deliver integrated instruction aimed at teaching high-level academic and technical content.
- *Students actively engaged:* Getting every student involved in rigorous and challenging learning.
- *Guidance:* Involving each student and his or her parents in a guidance and advising system that ensures the completion of an accelerated program of study with an in-depth academic or vocational-technical major.
- *Extra help:* Providing a structured system of extra help to enable students who may lack adequate preparation to complete an accelerated program of study that includes high-level academic and technical content.

- *Keeping score:* Using student assessment and program evaluation data to improve continuously the school climate, organization, management, curricula, and instruction to advance student learning and to recognize students who meet both curricular and performance goals. (Bottoms, 2002)

COMMITMENT TO BEST PRACTICES

Study of research literature and best practices are essential to building a viable transition program. One of the most beneficial elements to construction of a quality intervention is to visit and dialogue with people in the trenches. A site visit to an exemplary ninth-grade transition campus is invaluable in the inspiration phase of the project. Educational professionals connecting with and experiencing what others are doing is a significant meaningful activity with lasting impact. The concept of leaving no stone unturned in the quest for building an exceptional program with high probability of sustained long-term success is enhanced by site visits and continued engagement with other teaching professionals experiencing success on a daily basis. Carefully select and visit only those schools with hard data, both quantitative and qualitative, with successful long-range experience in implementing a ninth-grade transition program.

TEAM DEVELOPMENT

Campus teams are developed through time and the pain of compromises. During the stages that teams go through on the way to high performance they usually experience a growth process. Teams in the beginning or storming stage can move through the stages much more expediently with some training in individual personality differences and consensus building. Providing excellence in professional development is of supreme importance in lessening the pain and strife that teams of educational professionals and parents undergo in accomplishing team unity and commitment. Examples of some team-building development interventions include True Colors, Myers-Briggs Type Indicator, and Bi-Polar training. Immersion in activities that bring about the understanding of personal differences that inhibit or contribute to team interaction and diminish barriers to team productivity goes a long way toward attenuation of time-consuming team-building behaviors.

Professional educators reviewing literature related to change and implementation of new innovations in education should be a part of any professional development plan. Sustained reading of books such as Ken Blanchard's *Gung Ho, High Five,* and *The One Minute Manager Builds High Performance Teams* will contribute to the attitude of doing whatever it takes to facilitate success. One of the most beneficial books is entitled *Fish.* This book delineates four simple strategies that will, if implemented properly, improve any organization and professional educator team.

DEVELOPING COMMUNICATIONS

Of all the interventions mentioned in this book, improvement of both one- and two-way communications is the intervention that should be implemented first. The effort of providing telephones in the classroom should be at the top of every administrator's list. Second to that would be allocating time for teachers to provide both positive and constructive feedback about student progress to parents. A few phone calls a day from the school to home by teachers will make a significant contribution to building positive relationships between students, teachers, and parents. Communications should be two-way and collaborative between teachers and parents. The ultimate system for telecommunications would provide both voice and data with storage capabilities for voice mail and e-mail. This allows parents the convenience of asynchronous anytime and anywhere communications with educators. The best first step to creation of a high-quality educator and parent communications system for a ninth-grade transition initiative is development of daily phone or e-mail exchanges or both.

According to a survey developed by the North Central Regional Educational Laboratory (n.d.), the following list of items should be considered in developing a technology-based communications plan for parents and the community:

- Develop a portable community technology resource center that enables access to technology resources that support educational collaboration.

- Initiate a telecommunications tree maintained by volunteers to disseminate information to parents about the basics of operations of the portable technology resource center for improvement of students' learning achievement.
- Work in partnership with the community to organize technology access in remote locations throughout the school district.
- Afford technical support to stakeholders in establishing home computer and/or World Wide Web access as well as connection to district educational resources on the Internet.
- Establish a set of parent pages on the district website so that parents can get information about school activities. Provide access to homework, district employee e-mail addresses, district initiatives, and activities.
- Enlist the assistance of community members to volunteer as computer assistants to acquire higher-level technology skills.
- Develop a Web-based frequently asked questions or discussion area for parent/teacher communications to foster communications among interested educational stakeholders.
- Establish and maintain e-mail communications to facilitate the exchange of attachments or questions between teachers and parents in preparation for a conference.

Allowing parents to respond to survey questions such as those in the preceding list provides a wealth of information to utilize in the establishment of a telecommunications network to maximize resources in development of computer networking and Web development. The survey items should be tailored to the needs and network capabilities of the school and community; however, this list of survey items provides some interesting prompts for development of an instrument to measure parent/community technological needs and priorities.

TUTORIALS NETWORK

Student support and resource allocation, next to communications with parents, are of utmost importance. A primary difference between a successful student and an unsuccessful one is the ability to identify and utilize resources to enhance success. Successful students enlist the help of peers, teachers, or other resources to enhance their grades on homework and tests, while the unsuccessful students stand aside and hope for the best or just become apathetic.

The simplest and most inexpensive intervention that a school can implement to enhance student achievement is peer assistance or peer tutoring. Researching best practices in peer tutoring programs is worth the effort. By offering incentives such as time off, fast food coupons, local business freebies, and other creative perks, the innovative ninth-grade transition team can immediately affect student success and achievement in the positive direction. Peer assistance and tutoring enhances collaboration, improves school climate, and breaks barriers between successful and unsuccessful students with diverse backgrounds. Both groups benefit through the process, and high achievers are proven to achieve at even higher levels due to better retention of concepts and content material. Students involved in study buddies and peer tutoring also gain a considerable amount of improvement in self-concept or self-worth by contributing positively to such a program. If we had no money to build a transition program, this intervention would be the most important to implement for long-term gains. Being engaged in such a program in the past, it is easy to say that this is an absolutely essential component in ninth-grade transition. Connecting freshmen students with same-grade or older coaches, mentors, and peer tutors opens doors that have been closed for many years. The best-case scenario is that these doors will remain open into adult life for many students and one by one, students will become more successful and graduate.

REINFORCING "DOING WHATEVER IT TAKES"

All the interventions, successful practices, and commitments to change in the universe will go awry if the leaders in the educational organization fail to encourage and cultivate the "doing whatever it takes" attitude. Teachers must like what they are doing, be positively reinforced, and feel genuinely appreciated for their enduring efforts. Developing a social culture among educational professionals, support staff, and administration is imperative to foster growth and commitment. Positively reinforcing effort of teachers and staff by administrators builds trust and loyalty while making transition less stressful for all stakeholders.

Providing regular feedback and results related to extra efforts are small points on the map to success in implementation of ninth-grade and other reforms (figure 9.1). Expending the time to keep teachers, parents, and staff informed of progress toward targeted goals fosters support for projects or programs that require stress in implementation. Remembering to do the little things that educators appreciate can make

	What's in Place?	Where Are We Going?
Innovations, strategies, programs contributing to ninth-grade transition		
Communications systems with • Eighth-grade teachers • Eighth-grade staff • Eighth-grade students • Parents • Ninth-grade teachers • Ninth-grade staff community		
Strategies for maintaining communications with transitioning students and parents		
Approaches to implementing strategies targeted toward special needs populations		
Professional development of teachers and staff in research-based best practices and superior instructional strategies		
Strategies and approaches for continuous monitoring, evaluation, and adjustments to the plan		

Figure 9.1.   *Ninth-Grade Transition Planning Matrix*

or break the planned change. In research, recognition has been proven to be one of the most important forms of bolstering and maintaining progress. Money will not, benefits will not, nor will lavish vacations—the only motivational factors that contribute to improvement are recognition and reinforcement for effort expended toward improvement.

CONCLUSION

Pulling all these components, initiatives, and innovations together takes time and commitment. Implementing educational reforms does not happen over night or even in one year. The rewards of continuous efforts based on well-researched and implemented best practices that are tailored to the specific needs of a particular school come in increments. At times, the incremental progress may seem small or early on move in a negative direction; however, with positive attitudes, continuous monitoring, informed adjustments, and relentless pursuit of goals, expected progress will be inevitable.

REFERENCES

Bottoms, G. (2000). High schools that work. Retrieved from the Southern Regional Education Board website. Available online at www.sreb.org/Programs/*HSTW*/high.html [accessed September 1, 2002].

——. (2002). High schools that work: Key practices. Retrieved from the Southern Regional Education Board website. Available online at www.sreb.org/programs/hstw/background/keypractices.asp [accessed September 1, 2002].

LaPoint, V., W. Jordan, J. McPartland, and D. P. Towns. (1996). The talent development high school: Essential components. Report no. 1. Baltimore: Center for Research on the Education of Students Placed at Risk (CRESPAR), Johns Hopkins University.

North Central Regional Educational Laboratory. (n.d.). Tool no. 6: Parent technology survey. Retrieved from the North Central Regional Educational Laboratory website. Available online at www.ncrel.org/tplan/handbook/toolkt6.htm [accessed October 12, 2002].

School District of Greenville County Transition Committee. (2002). Meeting the challenge: The transition to and through ninth grade. Retrieved from the Greenville County South Carolina School District website. Available online at www.greenville.k12.sc.us/district/teachers/trans1.htm.

ADDITIONAL WEB RESOURCES

"Ninth Grade Success Academy." *Lawrence High School* (Lawrence, Mass.). www.lawrencepublicschools.org/Schools/LHS/Web/YTE1/9thgrade.htm. "The intent of this Ninth Grade Success Academy is to provide a more personalized and supportive academic environment for students while strengthening communication with parents."

"Ninth Grade Success Teams." *Arundel High School* (Gambrills, Md.). www.arundelhigh.org/academy/teams.html. "At Arundel High School for the 2002–2003 year, two separate Ninth Grade Success Teams (Smaller Learning Communities, or SLCs) were formed. Both are composed of a random group of students and a specifically chosen set of teachers to focus on the improvement of the Ninth Grade Program. The two teams direct positive efforts toward success for every A.H.S. student."

"Ninth Grade Success Initiative." *Round Rock High School* (Round Rock, Tex.). www.roundrockisd.org/rrhs/news/9thgradeinitiative.html. "Saturday Opportunity School Tutorials at Round Rock ISD have begun for current ninth graders and previous participants in the Ninth Grade Success Initiative. The program is funded by a grant from the Texas Education Agency. The purpose of the program is to prevent ninth graders from falling behind their class, because studies show that students who must repeat ninth grade are far more likely to drop out than are other students."

School District of Greenville County Transition Committee. "Meeting the Challenge: The Transition to and through Ninth Grade." www.greenville.k12.sc.us/district/teachers/trans1.htm. "One of the guiding premises in Greenville County's "Guide to Educational Excellence: Priorities for Performance" is that we must all work together to enable every student to achieve at high levels, pursue a lifetime of learning, and become an ethical, productive member of society."

Anderson, V. (1997). "Separate Buildings, Cluster Courses, Military Drills, Block Scheduling." *CATALYST: Voices of Chicago School Reform* 8(5). www.catalyst-chicago.org/02-97/027works.htm. "*CATALYST* Managing Editor Veronica Anderson visited five high schools that have embraced the practices that variously define a freshman academy. Some launched their efforts years ago, others as recently as last year."

Southern Regional Education Board (SREB). *High Schools That Work.* www.sreb.org/programs/hstw/hstwindex.asp. "High Schools That Work is the largest and oldest of the SREB's seven school-improvement initiatives for high-school and middle-grade leaders and teachers. More than 1,100 *HSTW* sites in twenty-seven states are using the *HSTW* framework of goals and key practices to raise student achievement."

Dykema, R. (2002). "How Schools Fail Kids and How They Could Be Better." *Nexus* (May/June). www.nexuspub.com/articles/2002/may2002/interview/2.htm. "This article features an interview with Kathy Simon of the Coalition of Essential Schools (CES)."

ERIC Clearinghouse on Educational Management. *Hot Topics.* eric.uoregon.edu/hot_topics/index.html. "ERIC has assembled resources on topics of high interest to many of their users."

Lezotte, L. "Revolutionary and Evolutionary: The Effective Schools Movement." *Effective Schools.* www.effectiveschools.com.

CHAPTER 10

Best Practices and Resources

A study of best practices reveals some exceptional and commendable efforts to save ninth-grade children from the perils of failure. Major emphasis is being placed on the creating and sharing of successful best practices that work in all schools. States are making concerted efforts to change the past practices of acceptable failure to a proactive approach to promoting student success. Accountability measures specifically targeted toward dropout or graduation rates are in place in some states and emerging in others. It is essential that best practices that tend to work across the nation be shared among the education communities. This chapter is a compilation of best practices and resources designed to help teachers, administrators, parents, and communities in construction of a plan that results in higher levels of student success as well as significant gains in graduation rates.

STATE-LEVEL INITIATIVES

In 1999, the 76th Texas Legislature allocated funds to support school districts' efforts to help ninth graders stay in school and succeed academically. Specifically, $42.5 million was appropriated for each year of the 2000–2001 biennium for implementation of the Ninth Grade Success Initiative (NGSI). The initiative provides resources that educators may use to design programs for at-risk ninth-grade students in their schools. Programs are expected to achieve four major objectives: (1) decrease the rate of retention in ninth grade, (2) reduce the number of ninth-grade dropouts, (3) increase attendance rates in ninth grade, and (4) support successful performance on the state's assessments, including the exit-level Texas Assessment of Academic Skills (Texas Education Agency, 2000).

TALENT DEVELOPMENT HIGH SCHOOL MODEL

The Talent Development High School model provides a change in paradigm from the long-established high school organizational structure. It focuses on the academy concept for ninth grade and stresses occupational pathways for grades 10–12. Professional educators from Patterson High School in Baltimore and an educational research team at Johns Hopkins University conceived, refined, and coined the model based on more rigorous curriculum, greater demands on students, and increased academic achievement. According to Jordan, Letgers, and McPartland (1998), the key components of the Talent Development model are as follows:

Primary Goals

The primary goal of the Talent Development model is to establish an effective model of secondary education in which all students, particularly those placed at risk, can succeed academically in an environment that supports rigorous curriculum, effective teaching strategies, and positive classroom climate.

Instructional Strategies and Materials

The Ninth Grade Success Academy focuses on the attendance and retention of ninth-grade students. The school day utilizes block scheduling, which offers teacher planning time. The Ninth Grade Academy is housed in a separate wing with its own classrooms, principal, and a faculty divided into interdisciplinary teams. The maximum size of the Ninth Grade Success Academy is 150–180 students.

Upper-Level Academies

Designed and instituted by school faculty and staff, career-focused academies draw on the strengths of school staff and student interest. The four Patterson High School career academies are Arts and Human-ities, Business and Finance, Sports Studies and Health/Wellness, and Transportation and Engineering Technology.

Improvement Grades and Credit School

The following programs provide academic support for students:

- Improvement Grades: This program allows students to earn extra report-card points.
- Credit School: For a small fee, students may participate in this after-school program, which permits them to make up missed credits.
- Twilight School: An alternative after-hours school for students who have disciplinary problems during the regular school day.
- Health Care: A full-service, professional clinic on-site to coordinate physical and mental services for students.

Participants

Patterson High School, the first site of the Talent Development model, is a neighborhood school of approximately 2,000 students. Sixty percent of the student body is African American, 30 percent is white, and 10 percent is American Indian, Asian American, and Latino.

Program Success

Initial research on the Talent Development Model High School was conducted at Patterson High School. Faculty surveys provided data on school climate and teaching conditions during the 1994–1995 and 1995–1996 school years. The surveys revealed the following findings:

- *Learning environment:* A marked change in teacher attitudes about the learning environment was evident before and after the implementation of the Talent Development model at Patterson. In fact, 86.7 percent of the upper-grade teachers and 80 percent of the ninth-grade teachers responded that the school environment was conducive to school achievement for most students. This was almost a complete reversal from the previous year, when 80 percent of the ninth-grade teachers and 87.6 percent of the upper-grade teachers believed the school environment was not conducive to learning.

- *Absenteeism:* Improved attendance rates were seen as a means of addressing overall school failure. In 1994–1995, teacher surveys showed that 96 percent of ninth-grade teachers and 97.8 percent of upper-level teachers agreed that absenteeism was a serious problem. After implementation of the Talent Development model, teacher surveys indicated that student behavior throughout the school had improved and class-cutting had decreased.

According to studies conducted by the Center for Research on the Education of Students Placed At Risk, the Johns Hopkins University Talent Development Model consists of four basic motivational factors students need in schools. Research on students at risk reveal a lack of support for the special circumstances of the students' economic, family, community, and minority status. Moreover, according to the U.S. Department of Education, Office of Educational Research and Improvement (1998), the following factors make up the research-based framework for the model:

- Relevance of schoolwork
- A caring and supportive human environment
- Opportunities for academic success
- Help with personal problems

Philadelphia Talent Development Schools

Philadelphia Public Schools implemented the Talent Development model at two high schools in the 1999–2000 school year. Students in the Philadelphia system were failing miserably. Less than 60 percent of ninth graders graduated from Philadelphia's public high schools within six years of entry (Philadelphia Education Fund, 2000).

According to the research reports by the Philadelphia Education Fund (2000) on the program, the specific components of the Talent Development Initiative were as follows:

- Intensive block scheduling in which students take only four eighty- to ninety-minute-period courses per semester
- A common-core college preparatory curriculum with double blocks of English and math
- A mandatory Freshman Seminar, Transition to Advanced Mathematics, and Strategic Reading courses in the fall semester
- Provision of intensive and subject-specific professional development for teachers and curriculum coaches with ongoing classroom-based implementation and support
- Self-contained career academies for grades ten through twelve, which provide a core academic curriculum, work-based learning, and career-focused pathway teams
- Emphasis on the use of student-centered teaching strategies such as teams and cooperative learning during longer periods
- Creation of after-hours Twilight School for students who have serious attendance and discipline problems or who come from detention facilities

To enhance teaching and administrative effectiveness, the following components were implemented as well:

- Data were utilized in an ongoing effort to provide feedback to teachers and administrators about the impact of the initiative.
- Organizational facilitators were provided to work full time at two high schools, assisting principals and staff with planning, data collection, changes in facilities, and leadership issues.
- Curricular coaches were provided for on-site professional development and in-class implementation support in the academic areas.
- Curricular materials were provided for first-term courses: Freshman Seminar, Strategic Reading, and Transition to Advanced Mathematics, and during the second term, there were supplementary materials for algebra and English.

According to data presented by the Philadelphia Education Fund (2000), the reform movement includes a significant decline in disciplinary suspensions from 125 to 37 at one site and from 1,049 to 788 at the other high school. The number of arrests decrease dramatically from a total of 187 to 37, indicating a tremendous new motivation to stay in school. Attendance improves slightly from an average of 69.5 percent to an average of 75 percent, which indicates that more work is needed in this area. The most significant increases occurred in the percentage of students promoted from ninth to tenth grade. Results indicate an increase in student promotion to tenth grade at the two schools from 47 to 65 percent the first year and from 65 to 75 percent in the two-year evaluation of the program. Standardized test scores in math also increase significantly in comparison with the control group. In light of the data and results, it is evident that the program is on the road to success and is worthy of investigation for implementation in other similar schools.

EFFECTIVE SCHOOLS

Efforts continue to implement the effective schools correlates across the nation even though the status of one of the nation's educational buzzwords has elapsed. The major focuses of the effective schools movement lives on today as viable research-based goals to improve schools. Perhaps the most important of the correlates today is establishing a school climate of high expectations and a professional teaching staff that not only buys into but exhibits teaching behaviors that contribute to students' mastery of the curriculum. Moreover, teachers should demonstrate the inherent behaviors that lead to high expectations and student success. They should truly become the walking and talking billboards for educational improvement, high expectation, positive climate, and learner-centered instruction. According to research and the effective schools philosophies of Lezotte (1991), simply raising the standards in a school does not necessarily equate to higher expectations for students. Furthermore, a world of difference exists between high standards and high expectations. High standards are the external factors that students are expected to meet, such as passing standards and graduation requirements. An expectation is the internal belief held by the adults that the kids can and will meet those higher standards. Expectations are crucial (Lezotte, 1991).

CLASS SIZE

Of all the innovations, interventions, and educational improvements discussed in this book, the one that is most likely to make significant gains in the shortest period of time is the reduction of the student-to-teacher ratio. Through years of continuous research, class size has proven to be one of the most predictive factors in student success and achievement. However, reducing the number of students in classes proves to be one of the most costly measures undertaken in the quest for improvement. Professional teaching salaries and benefits equate to over 80 percent of every school budget, and adding more teachers is essential to reduction of class size. The current trends in educational funding make it necessary to be very creative in assignment of personnel to maximize the reduction of class size. Although it is a costly measure, administrators should explore every possible path, leaving no stone unturned, to develop a plan for reducing the number of students assigned per teacher.

Small schools consistently outperform large urban schools, and the fact that teachers know the children, their parents, and the specific problems of community life contributes to this success. Large schools are moving toward development of smaller communities of learning within the confines of oversized urban schools in an attempt to create the same atmosphere afforded in smaller rural schools.

According to Pritchard (1999), the pattern of findings drawn from the existing research leads to three conclusions: First, class-size reduction in the early grades creates greater levels of student achievement, and significant effects on student achievement emerge when class size is reduced to between fifteen and twenty students. Achievement continues to increase as class size moves toward the one-to-one tutorial. Second, research from the pertinent studies shows that if class size is reduced from considerably more than twenty students to less than twenty students, student achievement improves for the average student from the 50th percentile to upward of the 60th percentile. These data also support the premise that disadvantaged and at-risk students benefit at even higher levels. Conclusively, students, teachers, and parents all report the affirmative impact of class-size reductions on excellence in classroom activity.

Research conducted by Finn (1998), on Tennessee's Student–Teacher Achievement Ratio (STAR) Project supports a number of improvements that are likely to occur when class-size reduction is implemented. It is noted that students in small classes were less disruptive than peers in larger classes. In addition, fewer kindergarten through grade one students were retained in the smaller classes. Pupils who had been in small classes were rated as expending more effort in the classroom, taking greater initiative with regard to learning activities, and displaying less disruptive or inattentive behavior compared with their peers who had been in regular-size classes (Finn, 1998).

Reducing class sizes to less than twenty students has the potential to significantly improve and positively influence student achievement. Though a costly endeavor, longitudinal research indicates that class-size reduction yields significantly favorable results in student achievement. A multitude of ways and means exist to implement reduction of class size. In addition, a significant number of innovative ideas are available to prepare teachers to deliver instruction in small classes. In essence, the fruits of the labor expended in reducing class size will be directly proportional to the quality of the effort and planning for the reduction program.

CONCLUSION

A plethora of innovations, resources, and successful best practices exist in education today, which can fundamentally change the pattern of continued student failure, grade-level retention, and high dropout rates. Schools need to make a conscious effort to craft plans of action targeted at improving the learning environments in and out of schools that foster a significant change in education for the large numbers of ninth-grade students in this country. Beginning with research and visits to sites where improvement efforts are significantly influencing student success, teams of professional educators and parents should develop action plans to implement proven practices that have a high probability of success in the first year as well as long term. Constant monitoring and evaluation of the plan, along with periodic adjustments, will be necessary to sustain improvement in the graduation rates of students. Through exploration and exploitation of all available resources, implementation of a quality endeavor will have a great potential to improve education for ninth-grade students. Ninth grade is truly a pivotal year, and a long-term commitment is required to realize significant gains in this area; we must take the steps to stop this titanic problem facing so many public schools. The pie-in-the-sky idea of every child moving past grade nine, in only one year, can become a reality through collaborative efforts of interested educators, community members, and parents.

REFERENCES

Finn, J. (1998). Class size and students at risk: What is known? What is next? Retrieved from the United States Department of Education website. Available online at www.ed.gov/pubs/ClassSize/ [accessed October 12, 2002].

Jordan, W., N. Letgers, and J. McPartland. (1998). Effects on teachers and students after two years in a Talent Development High School. Center report. Baltimore: Center for Research on the Education of Students Placed at Risk (CRESPAR), Johns Hopkins University.

Lezotte, L. W. (1991). Correlates of effective schools: The first and second generation. Okemos, Mo.: Effective Schools Products.

Philadelphia Education Fund. (2000). The talent development high school: First-year results of the Ninth Grade Success Academy in two Philadelphia schools, 1999–2000. Retrieved from the Philadelphia Education Fund website. Available online at www.philaedfund.org [accessed September 2, 2002].

Pritchard, I. (1999). Reducing class size: What do we know? National Institute on Student Achievement, Curriculum and Assessment. Office of Educational Research and Improvement, U.S. Department of Education.

Texas Education Agency. (2000). Ninth grade success initiative grants awarded to 234 school districts and consortiums. Press release retrieved from the Texas Education Agency website. Available online at www.tea.state.tx.us/press/pr000125.html [accessed October 5, 2002].

U.S. Department of Education, Office of Educational Research and Improvement. (1998). Tools for schools: School reform models supported by the national institute on the education of at-risk students. Washington, D.C. Retrieved from the United States Department of Education website. Available online at www.ed.gov/pubs/ToolsforSchools/title.html [accessed September 17, 2002].

ADDITIONAL WEB RESOURCES

Center for Social Organization of Schools, Johns Hopkins University. www. csos.jhu.edu/tdhs/index.htm. "The first Talent Development High School was established in September 1995 at Patterson High School in Baltimore. The model at Patterson incorporates career-focused academies for the upper grades, a ninth-grade academy with teams of teachers and students, and other key Talent Development components."

Center for Research on the Education of Students Placed at Risk (CRESPAR). "Talent Development High School." depts.washington.edu/centerme/talent. htm#abstract. "The Talent Development High School restructures the traditional high-school model through the creation of smaller career-focused academies for the upper grades (10–12) and a ninth-grade academy."

Texas Education Agency. (2000). "Ninth Grade Success Initiative Grants Awarded to 234 School Districts and Consortiums." www.tea.state.tx.us/ press/pr000125.html. "The goal of the Texas Education Agency's program, also known as the Ninth Grade Success Initiative, is to increase graduation rates in Texas public schools by reducing the number of students who are retained in the ninth grade or who drop out that year."

University of Texas at Austin, Office of Public Affairs. (1999). "Ninth-Grade Success Initiative: Focus on Mathematics and Science." www.utexas.edu/ admin/opa/news/99newsreleases/nr_199910/nr_dana991007.html. "To receive Ninth Grade Success Initiative (NGSI) funding, subsection (a) of Texas Education Code § 29.086 stipulates that programs must target ninth graders who have not earned—or are not likely to earn—sufficient credit to advance to tenth grade and who fail to meet minimum skill levels. Also, according to that law's subsection (b), NGSI programs must emphasize basic skills in core curricular areas and provide targeted students with opportunities to build credits toward graduation."

U.S. Department of Education. (1999). "Reducing Class Size: What Do We Know?" www.ed.gov/pubs/ReducingClass/. "According to this report, which summarizes research on class size, 'Significant effects of class size reduction on student achievement appear when class size is reduced to a point between 15 and 20 students.'"

U.S. Department of Education. (1998). "Class Size and Students at Risk: What Is Known? What Is Next?" www.ed.gov/pubs/ClassSize/. "This report reviews research on class size, discusses approaches taken to assess the costs and benefits of reducing class size, and explores implications of smaller classes for classroom management and instructional strategies, particularly for students at risk."

Web66: A K12 World Wide Web Project. web66.coled.umn.edu/. "This site will help teachers see the World Wide Web as a catalyst to assist in the integration of the Internet into K12 school curricula. The Web66 site was designed to make introduction of this technology into K12 schools easier and pain free."

"Staff Development Standards Checklist." Based on National Staff Development Council Staff Development Standards. www.nsdc.org/list.htm. "Visit this site to view the National Staff Development Council's checklist of staff development standards for public schools."

No Child Left Behind resources from the National Staff Development Council. www.nsdc.org/educatorindex.htm. "Contents of this site include the information resources in the National Staff Development Council (NSDC) library and covers the No Child Left Behind Act, with recent articles from NSDC publications and websites from the U.S. Department of Education and other organizations."

U.S. Department of Education. *No Child Left Behind.* www.nochildleftbehind. gov/. "At the U.S. Department of Education's *No Child Left Behind* website, learn about the *Education News Parents Can Use* television series, powerful new tools to help children learn and achieve, supplemental services, charter schools and testing, and the basics of the No Child Left Behind legislation."

U.S. Department of Education. Full text of the legislation: No Child Left Behind. www.ed.gov/legislation/ESEA02/. "Access and read the full-text legislation of the No Child Left Behind (NCLB) Act. This site contains a table of contents that links to each section of the NCLB legislation."

U.S. Department of Education, Office of the Under Secretary. (2002). *No Child Left Behind: A Desktop Reference.* www.ed.gov/offices/OESE/reference.pdf. "The U.S. Department of Education has provided a 181-page desktop reference, in Acrobat Reader format, of the NCLB Act. This Web document contains a shortened explanation of all the components of the legislation."

Index

applying the brakes checklist, 44
assessing: staff, 13; students, 13
attendance, lowest, 4
attitude, 63

best practices, 99–106; class size, 105; effective schools, 104; impact of, 106; state-level initiatives, 99; Student–Teacher Achievement Ratio, 106

change process, 57
communications: calls per week, 24; email, 25; parcel post, 26–27; parent, 92; phones in the classroom, 23–24; team script, 32; telephone conversation plan, 31; web, 26. *See also* conferences; developing communications
conferences, 27–28; advanced preparation, 28; checklist for effective, 30; effective conferencing, 29; training, 29–30, 41
connection with adults, 39

developing communications, 91–92; one-way, 91; two-way, 91–92
developing the program, 86–88
diagnosis, 43
doing whatever it takes, 58; checklist, 59; reinforcing, 93
dropouts, 5

empowering, teachers, 40
extended-day learning, 66
extended-year learning, 66–67

grading, practices, 16

High Schools That Work initiative, 88–90

mastery learning, 67–69
mentoring, 79
motivation: student, 17, 42; teachers, 41

organizational attitude, 59
orientation, 38

About the Author

Robert L. Marshall is an associate professor of education and director of the joint university doctoral program in educational leadership at Texas A&M University–Kingsville, a Carnegie Doctoral Intensive institution in the South Texas region. He serves as chair of the Texas A&M University–Kingsville graduate council and was selected as the outstanding faculty member in the TAMUK College of Education in 2000. This is his first book on ninth-grade transition and student success.

He was a public school teacher, campus principal, and central office administrator in Texas public schools for twenty years. Throughout his career as a professional educator, the issue of research and best practices in creating a high-quality learning environment for students in transition to high school has been a passion.

Marshall holds a doctor of education degree from Texas A&M University, principalship certification from the University of Texas–Tyler, master of science degree in agriculture from Texas A&M University–Commerce, and a bachelor of science degree in agriculture education from East Texas State University. His other publications include *Educational Leadership in a Nutshell: A Guide to Comprehensive Exam Success* (2001) as well as its second edition (2002).